Small-Group Reading Instruction

A Differentiated Teaching Model for Beginning and Struggling Readers

BEVERLY TYNER

Hamilton County Schools
Chattanooga, Tennessee, USA

INTERNATIONAL
Reading Association
800 Barksdale Road, PO Box 8139
Newark, DE 19714-8139, USA
www.reading.org

KH

The International Reading Association attempts, through its publications, to provide a forum for a wide spectrum of opinions on reading. This policy permits divergent viewpoints without implying the endorsement of the Association.

Director of Publications Joan M. Irwin
Editorial Director, Books and Special Projects Matthew W. Baker
Managing Editor Shannon Benner
Permissions Editor Janet S. Parrack
Acquisitions and Communications Coordinator Corinne M. Mooney
Associate Editor, Books and Special Projects Sara J. Murphy
Assistant Editor Charlene M. Nichols
Administrative Assistant Michele Jester
Senior Editorial Assistant Tyanna L. Collins
Production Department Manager Iona Muscella
Supervisor, Electronic Publishing Anette Schütz
Senior Electronic Publishing Specialist Cheryl J. Strum
Electronic Publishing Specialist R. Lynn Harrison
Proofreader Elizabeth C. Hunt

Project Editor Charlene M. Nichols

Cover Design, Linda Steere; Photographs, Beverly Tyner and Fred Carr

Web addresses in this book were correct as of the publication date but may have become inactive or otherwise modified since that time. If you notice a deactivated or changed Web address, please e-mail books@reading.org with the words "Website Update" in the subject line. In your message, specify the Web link, the book title, and the page number on which the link appears.

Library of Congress Cataloging-in-Publication Data
Tyner, Beverly.
Small-group reading instruction : a differentiated teaching model for beginning and struggling readers / Beverly Tyner.
p. cm.
Includes bibliographical references and index.
ISBN 0-87207-007-7
1. Reading (Elementary) 2. Group reading. 3. Reading—Remedial teaching.
I. Title.
LB1573.T96 2003
372.41'62–dc22

2003016451

Seventh Printing, June 2006

10/19/06

To my mother, Helen Davis Bernard, who remains a champion for the "struggling reader" and most of all a champion for her family

CONTENTS

FOREWORD

Dr. Beverly Tyner is a very determined woman. I met her in 1997 when she convinced me to come to Chattanooga, Tennessee, USA, to help her set up an early reading intervention program in the city's public schools. That year, Beverly, already a full-time curriculum coordinator in the school system, shadowed me on each of my nine consultation visits, and she tutored a struggling first-grade reader every day after school. I had never before met a school administrator with such a burning commitment to learn about and to improve reading instruction for at-risk children. In just two years, she helped establish successful reading intervention programs in 10 economically disadvantaged schools in the city.

Although I kept in touch with Beverly, I had little idea of how she had spent her time professionally; therefore, I was quite surprised when she informed me this past spring that she had just completed a book on the small-group teaching of reading. She explained that she had taken the tutoring principles in my intervention program (Early Steps) and adapted them for small-group use in the classroom. Moreover, she had field-tested the instructional ideas in kindergarten and first- and second-grade classrooms and knew that they worked. I believed her.

Beverly succeeds in melding well-known teaching techniques, such as Early Steps and Reading Recovery, with a sophisticated theory of early reading development in *Small-Group Reading Instruction: A Differentiated Teaching Model for Beginning and Struggling Readers*. To my knowledge, it is unique. Teachers who read this book will learn not only about the stages of beginning reading but also how to assess, plan, instruct, and manage within the constraints of a busy classroom. They will find the book to be eminently practical but also driven by a strong—and in my opinion—accurate developmental theory.

Not all reading educators will agree with Beverly's perspective on beginning reading. Some will find it too skill oriented; others will find it lacking in this regard. This is to be expected in a complex and contentious field in which trends come and go with the changing of the decades. However, I believe practitioners will welcome Beverly's instructional model, which features a blend of meaningful contextual reading, systematic word study, and writing. They also will welcome her developmentally oriented advice on *when*, *why*, and *how* to provide instruction to beginning and struggling readers.

Kindergarten, first-, and second-grade teachers face enormous challenges in providing effective reading instruction. Most realize that some type of differentiation or grouping is needed if all children's needs are to be met; nonetheless, how to proceed once the students are grouped has always been a daunting problem. This book provides theory-based, practical guidance in this important area. If it is read, interpreted, and applied by classroom teachers as Beverly intended, then many children in our schools will benefit from its publication.

Darrell Morris
Appalachian State University
Boone, North Carolina, USA

PREFACE

My purpose in writing this book is to present an effective small-group differentiated reading model for teachers who work with beginning readers in kindergarten through grade 2 or struggling readers through grade 5. In my almost 30 years as a teacher, principal, reading specialist, and college professor, I have worked in three large urban school districts and two universities across three states in the southeastern United States. My primary observation in these varied experiences has been the desperate needs of both students and teachers in the area of beginning reading instruction. Many teachers and students continue to be saddled with ineffective reading instruction driven by basal reading adoptions. Teachers are left unsupported in the training and materials necessary to teach beginning reading, and students are left to struggle.

Effective reading instruction comprises guided contextual reading and systematic word study that is skillfully paced to the rate of individual students. This type of teaching and learning is most effective when instruction is delivered in the smallest group possible so as to best address the specific literacy needs of the students. Providing such instruction in primary classrooms, which often range from 24 to 28 students, is increasingly difficult. Basal readers provide only capable readers with an appropriate text and accompanying word study—usually delivered in whole-class instruction. In my work with thousands of teachers across the United States, I have found that most feel that their college training did not fully prepare them for the wide range of readers in their classrooms who are left struggling in the basal program.

Tutorial programs such as Reading Recovery (Clay, 1993) and Early Steps (Morris, Tyner, & Perney, 2000) have been successful with individual students in schools where sufficient funds have been available. Students in these programs typically are taken out of the classroom and given 30 minutes of one-on-one instruction on a daily basis. However, a comparable model for small-group instruction in the regular classroom setting has been lacking. There is no question that one-on-one tutoring provides the most effective instruction for struggling readers (Morris et al., 2000; Santa, 1999), but additional quality instruction for all children in the classroom setting is necessary for maximum growth.

For the past 11 years, I have focused my attention on the development of a comprehensive reading model that would provide effective beginning reading instruction for all students. Although I have a great deal of respect for the complexities of reading and writing and the research that surrounds it, my primary concerns in writing this book are simplicity and usability. Having carefully reviewed the research that surrounds this important topic, I am confident that the Small-Group Differentiated Reading Model is intrinsically steeped in the best practices in beginning reading instruction. Perhaps more important, I know that these strategies work, as evidenced in research (Morris et al., 2000; Santa, 1999) as well as in the daily successes of the students I have observed participating in this model.

Small-Group Reading Instruction: A Differentiated Teaching Model for Beginning and Struggling Readers can be used for a variety of purposes. Although intended primarily for use by classroom teachers in kindergarten through second grade and by reading specialists, it also can provide a solid basis for reading instruction in teacher training programs. Finally, this book can be used in reading intervention programs with individuals or small groups of beginning or struggling readers throughout the elementary school grades.

It is my sincere hope that the Small-Group Differentiated Reading Model will assist teachers in attaining the goal of making every child a competent reader.

ACKNOWLEDGMENTS

During the 1997–1999 school years, it was my great pleasure to work alongside Darrell Morris, professor of reading at Appalachian State University, as he trained reading tutors in my school district. His work is the guiding force behind my efforts in writing this book. Along with his extensive knowledge of the reading process, Darrell brings a personal dedication to providing effective reading instruction to all beginning readers. Darrell and I conducted a research study that documented the success of his reading intervention model, Early Steps, in a large urban district (Morris et al., 2000). Much of the information in this book is based on the work of Darrell, whose sincere desire to share with others brings a rare authenticity to his craft.

I cannot overlook the hundreds of teachers who have worked with me over the past years in perfecting this model. Their excitement and dedication to the teaching of reading inspires me on a daily basis and motivated me to publish this book. It is, I am convinced, in the "everydayness" of the classroom that real research takes place.

I also would like to thank my husband, Paul, for his patience and support as I worked on this project, and my four precious children (Leslie, Susan, Jennifer, and Harrison) who taught me a great deal about the reading process. I feel certain they will be pleased that they will no longer have to ask, "Are you still working on that book?"

Most important, I want to thank the many children who unknowingly participated in the development of this book. Their daily successes and struggles are the basis of this text. It is in the faces of these children—as they find success and pleasure in learning to read—that I see a brighter future unfold for each one of them. If this work touches the life of only one child, it was well worth the effort.

CHAPTER 1

Beginning Reading Instruction and the Small-Group Differentiated Reading Model

Over the past decade, there has been an unprecedented focus on the teaching of beginning reading. Teachers are passionate about early reading success because they know that it is the cornerstone upon which knowledge, self-esteem, and future educational opportunities are built. Literacy standards are on the rise, and those students who fail to reach high literacy levels are doomed to failure both educationally and economically. Research is clear about the need for early, effective reading instruction. Clay (1985) found that low-performing first-grade readers will likely be the lowest performing readers in the fourth grade. If teachers are to make high literacy levels a reality for all children, the instruction must begin when students enter the schoolhouse door. Although teachers know a great deal about the reading process, many questions remain concerning the most effective methods to use when instructing children. I have encountered many teachers who are frustrated by the lack of quality materials available for beginning reading instruction. Moreover, these teachers often comment that they were poorly prepared in their undergraduate training to meet the needs of beginning and struggling readers in their classrooms. The Small-Group Differentiated Reading Model presented in this book will give each student a chance to receive the reading instruction he or she deserves. In addition to addressing student needs, the model also supports teachers by presenting an easy-to-implement instructional model that incorporates research-based strategies essential to early literacy success.

Children begin their formal literacy journey when they enter school, whether it is a preschool or kindergarten program. Beginning this journey requires teachers to assess each student's literacy knowledge and provide the appropriate instruction that will advance the child's literacy learning. Students enter a typical kindergarten class with very different levels of printed language knowledge, and instruction must be adapted for these differences. Implementing the components of balanced literacy instruction, including small-group reading, is an effective way to provide appropriate instruction. Some educators feel that teacher-directed reading is inappropriate for young children. On the contrary, young children deserve the same literacy opportunities as older children. Numerous young children are often left behind when they fail to acquire skills and knowledge critical to literacy development such as the ability to track print, alphabet knowledge, and phonemic awareness. Traditionally, instruction in these areas has taken place in a whole-class setting with little regard for individual student needs.

Beyond the Basal for Beginning Readers

Basal reading programs are the dominant means of reading instruction in the United States. *Webster's Ninth New Collegiate Dictionary* defines *basal* as "bottom; part of a thing on which it rests; foundation; support; starting place" (1984, p. 92). This describes the appropriate role of a basal text: A basal reading series was never meant to provide a complete program, only a starting point. Basal readers are most effective when they are used flexibly and as part of a comprehensive, balanced program of instruction. Conversely, basal readers are least effective when they are used as the total reading program. This is true of all levels of readers but has particular implications for beginning readers.

The most overlooked component in current basal series is small-group reading in appropriately leveled texts. Although some basal programs give lip service to small-group instruction, the materials and guides necessary for successful implementation are often lacking. It is not advantageous for textbook companies to support an extensive small-group reading model that requires school districts to purchase numerous books because it would be cost prohibitive. Textbook companies are in a competitive market, and, therefore, they try to present the most economical program. However, without carefully leveled reading materials to supplement the basal, it is impossible to meet the needs of beginning and struggling readers.

Children in the early stages of literacy development have unique needs. If children are to seek hungrily for literacy, they must experience early success in beginning reading. Typically, the basal reader covers one story a week. Limiting a child to reading one story a week—a text that may or may not be at the appropriate instructional level—limits the child's ability to reach higher levels of achievement. According to Betts (1946), the "instructional level" of reading is the highest level at which a student can read with support from the teacher. Reading and rereading a variety of texts at appropriate levels drives instruction forward for all students.

Perhaps the group most neglected in a basal-only reading program is struggling readers. High achievers are capable of reading the weekly story before it is introduced; therefore, these students flourish in spite of the system. Average students probably fare best within the basal reading model, although they too are limited by reading opportunities. Struggling readers, on the other hand, are the clear losers in a basal-only classroom. More often than not, their only reading instruction is presented at a level of frustration—the level at which they cannot comfortably succeed. This then begins the downward spiral; motivation is lost and the gap between readers and nonreaders widens.

Gaps in the Guided Reading Model

Significant attention has been given to guided reading in recent years. The developers of guided reading, Fountas and Pinnell (1996), should be applauded for their contributions to this important reading process. It has, in fact, been the only reading model that has attempted to instruct children in a small group at an appropriate instructional reading level. The goal of the guided reading model is "to help children learn how to use independent reading strategies successfully" (p. 2), which focuses primarily on comprehension strategies. It could, therefore, be interpreted that this type of guided reading is most appropriate for those students who already have mastered basic decoding skills such as concepts of print, letter sounds, sight words, or basic phonics and have reached somewhat independent reading levels. Although the ultimate goal of any reading program is to comprehend text, basic foundational decoding skills cannot be overlooked. Do we magically hand a book to a nonreader and say "read"? For many beginning and struggling readers it is not that simple. What happens to those readers who lack the prerequisite skills that are needed for reading? Many beginning readers require focused instruction that includes alphabet knowledge, phonics, or even the ability to track simple lines of print. It is our responsibility as teachers to determine the developmental needs of each student in the beginning reading process and offer instruction necessary to advance his or her literacy learning.

Although Fountas and Pinnell present some excellent comprehension strategies, there are some deficits in this model that cannot be ignored for beginning and struggling readers. The accompanying systematic word study, writing, and oral reading strategies are necessary to complete the literacy framework. Figure 1 shows the similarities and differences between guided reading and the Small-Group Differentiated Reading Model presented in this book. Although it might be argued that word study and writing are taught during another part of the school day, the effectiveness of this instruction in the context of whole-class instruction with little regard for individual needs is questionable. Until a child becomes an independent reader, word study and writing

FIGURE 1
Comparing Guided Reading and the Small-Group Differentiated Reading Model

Guided Reading	Small-Group Differentiated Reading Model
Students grouped according to reading level	Students grouped according to reading and word study level
Uses leveled books	Uses leveled books
Comprehension focus	Decoding and comprehension focus
Each child reads the whole text	Variety of reading strategies used (oral, silent, partner, and choral reading)
No systematic word study component	Systematic word study (beginning with alphabet knowledge and continuing through variant vowel patterns)
No writing component	Writing (beginning with shared writing and progressing to independent writing)
No word bank	Word bank (automatic recognition of basic sight words)

are so closely linked in the developmental reading process that they are most effectively taught in a systematic way that supports each child's reading level and builds a solid decoding as well as comprehension foundation. Although traditional guided reading has much to offer, we cannot ignore potential instructional gaps for beginning readers. As a parent, teacher, administrator, and reading specialist, I have observed that a more explicit small-group reading model is necessary for beginning and struggling readers.

The Small-Group Differentiated Reading Model

Development of the Model

My interest in developing a specific small-group differentiated reading model resulted from my work as a reading specialist in a large urban school district in the southeastern United States. Along with other urban districts, our district was experiencing an ever-increasing number of students reading below grade level. In an attempt to reduce these reading failures, a search began for an early, intensive reading intervention model that could assist numerous students. The Reading Recovery model (Clay, 1993) was quickly ruled out because of the program's high cost and inability to serve more than a few students dictated by the program guidelines. However, Early Steps, a reading intervention model developed by Darrell Morris, met the criteria. Reading tutors, assistants, and volunteers could be trained in this early intervention model, and numerous at-risk students could be served.

Early Steps, a one-on-one tutoring intervention, is based on research and best practices in reading instruction, including rereading, word study, and writing as integral parts. Most important, reading tutors are trained on site in an apprenticeship format. First-grade students in our district made impressive gains as a result of the implementation of Early Steps (see Morris et al., 2000). Although the intervention was successful for individual students, the basal reading program continued to be ineffective in meeting the needs of students in the classroom. Whole-class instruction and a lack of appropriately leveled books left teachers frustrated.

Using the components of Early Steps, I set out to develop a small-group differentiated instructional model that would address the needs of beginning and struggling readers in the regular classroom setting. The Small-Group Differentiated Reading Model (see Figure 2) provides a systematic framework for teaching beginning and struggling readers. It takes into consideration the developmental stages through which readers progress, the critical strategies for reading success, and the time needed to develop these literacy foundations.

What Is Differentiated Reading Instruction?

As many schools move toward adapting to an ever-increasing broad range of learners, it becomes more important than ever to develop instruction to respond to these academically diverse students. Research has documented the tendency of educators to

FIGURE 2
The Small-Group Differentiated Reading Model

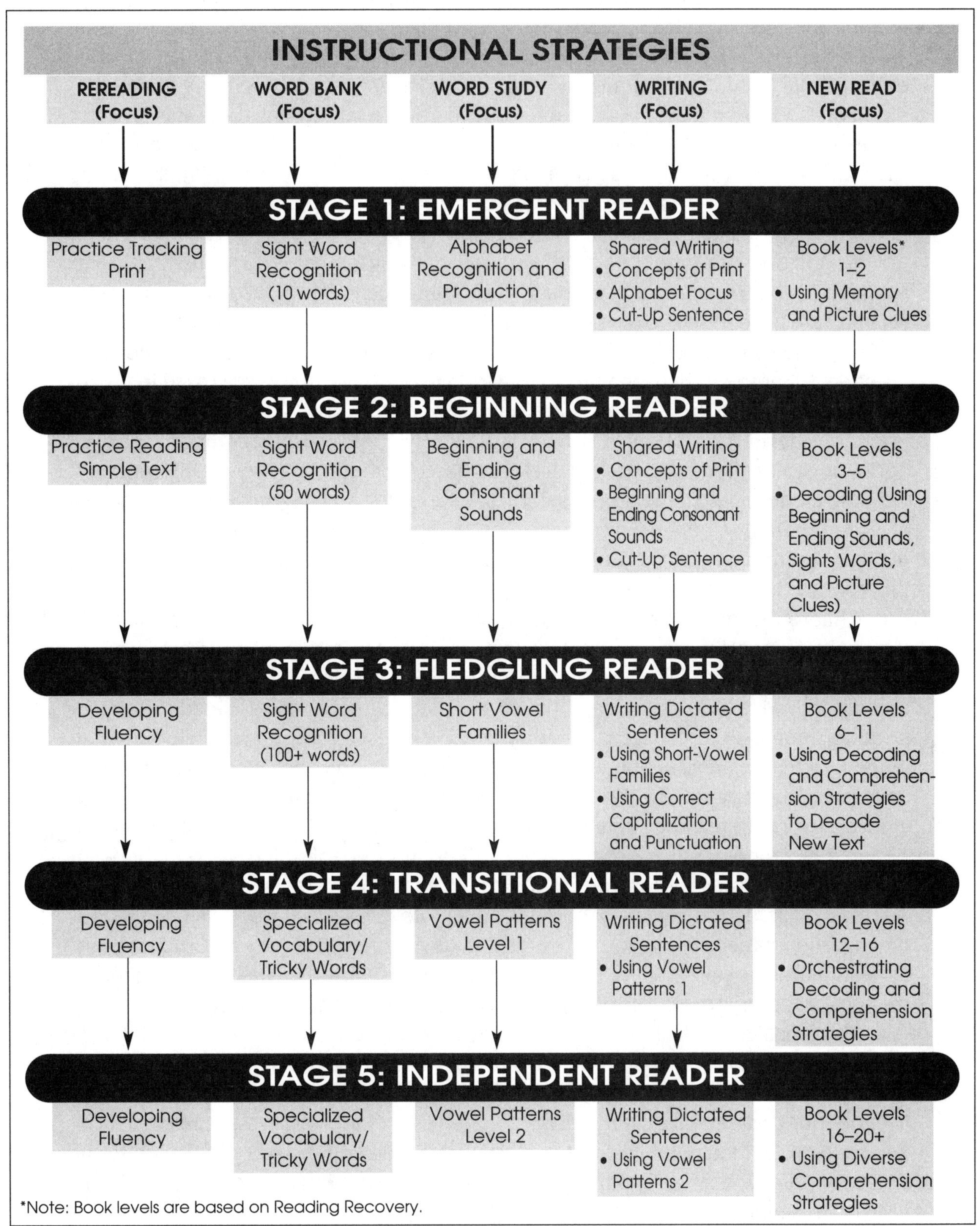

"teach to the middle," or to "teach to a standard" (see, for example, Darling-Hammond & Goodwin, 1993). This one-size-fits-all curriculum has failed to meet the needs of many slower and accelerated students. Differentiating instruction for beginning readers is one step to appropriately address the academic diversity that exists in virtually every primary classroom. Quite simply, differentiation means modifying instruction based on student readiness. A research study in Texas revealed that there was typically a four-year grade span between the lowest and highest readers in first-grade classrooms (Guszak, as cited in Texas Reading Initiative: Differentiated Instruction). Differentiating reading instruction enables teachers to plan strategically so that they can meet the needs of both weaker and stronger students.

At its core, the model of differentiated reading presented in this book uses research-based strategies in beginning reading instruction and developmental models that recognize the stages through which beginning readers must progress. Readers and nonreaders have been typically categorized as either one group or the other with little regard for the in-between group in which many beginning and struggling readers are often trapped. Reading is not an all-or-nothing skill: Alphabet knowledge, phonemic awareness, phonics, print-related knowledge, word recognition, spelling, and writing are all integral parts. This is the basis for the Small-Group Differentiated Reading Model. The question then becomes, Where along the reading continuum does each reader fall? Whenever a teacher reaches out to a small reading group to vary teaching techniques and strategies to create the best teaching experience possible, differentiated instruction takes place.

Children enter the classroom with a variety of background experiences. For children with lots of prior experiences with print, many of the early reading processes may already be mastered. In contrast, children who enter with relatively no knowledge about print will require a different instructional plan. Without differentiated reading instruction, some children will fall further behind whereas others will be left unchallenged. In reading instruction, the gap between poor and good readers widens with each subsequent year (Clay, 1985). The Small-Group Differentiated Reading Model includes a variety of reading strategies based on the developmental needs of the reader, not on the chronological age or grade level. Although student differences might be inconvenient at times to accommodate, they must be recognized and addressed. Adapting to student diversity is the price educators must pay if we are sincere about having students achieve higher standards and having the best interest of each student at heart. Students start at different points in the reading process, and we must provide the most appropriate level of challenge to increase their literacy learning.

The Small-Group Differentiated Reading Model presented in Figure 2 is differentiated in two important ways. First, the five stages in the beginning reading process—emergent reader, beginning reader, fledgling reader, transitional reader, and independent reader—are clearly differentiated as a reader progresses toward independence. Additionally, the instructional strategies—rereading, word bank, word study, writing, and new read—are differentiated: They support both code-emphasis (phonics) and meaning-emphasis (whole language) strategies. Although there remains some contention concerning these two predominant methods of reading instruction, it is time to recognize the common ground that research clearly supports: a need for both strategies to be taught.

Differentiating the Stages of Beginning Reading

Reading is a complex process with many steps and variables. However, the road to reading has some definite milestones through which readers must navigate. According to *Webster's Ninth New Collegiate Dictionary*, the definition of *differentiation* is "the development of the simple to the complex" (1984, p. 205). Additionally, *Webster's* defines the word as "a difference between individuals of the same kind." Beginning readers are often lumped together with little delineation of differences, yet these differences are critical to the reading process and should not be ignored.

To differentiate also means "to vary according to circumstance" (*Oxford Illustrated American Dictionary*, 1998, p. 227). In most primary classrooms, some students struggle with reading, others perform well beyond grade-level expectations, and the rest fall somewhere in between. By differentiating the stages of reading instruction through flexible small groups, the diverse needs of a heterogeneous group can best be met. This differentiated reading model recognizes the developmental stages through which a reader progresses and adapts instructional strategies to support the reader in each stage. Allowing for flexible small-group reading instruction in primary classrooms where some students struggle and others perform well beyond grade-level expectations provides appropriate instruction for all readers.

To effectively guide the reading process, first there must be an understanding of the stages in beginning reading and the print demands placed on a reader at these different stages. For example, in the early stages of reading, there is a heavier emphasis on decoding than on comprehension. Contextual reading, writing, spelling, sight-word recognition, and phonics develop simultaneously in predictable stages. Figure 3 details the five stages that are addressed in the Small-Group Differentiated Reading Model. Appropriate grade-level designations are given for each of the reading stages along with the beginning student characteristics and major focuses of each stage. This progression begins in Stage 1 with the emergent reader (basically nonreader) and continues to an independent reading level in Stage 5. Students advance through these levels as they build on their knowledge and move forward at their own pace. These five stages serve as the basis for the Small-Group Differentiated Reading Model presented in this book and will be discussed thoroughly in chapters 4 through 8.

Differentiating Instructional Strategies

Over the past decades, many educators and parents have become frustrated with or confused about the wide swings in the reading instruction pendulum. A team of U.S. national education associations recently observed,

FIGURE 3
Stages of Beginning Reading

Stage	Appropriate Grade Level	Beginning Student Characteristics	Major Focuses
1 Emergent Reader	Pre-K/K	• Knows less than half the alphabet • Has no concept of word • Has little phonemic awareness • Recognizes a few sight words	• Using memory and pictures • Recognizing and reproducing letters of the alphabet • Tracking print • Distinguishing beginning consonant sounds • Recognizing 10 sight words
2 Beginning Reader	Late K/ Early First Grade	• Knows three quarters or more of the alphabet • Is beginning to track print • Is able to hear some sounds • Recognizes 10 sight words	• Completing alphabet recognition and production • Using beginning and ending consonant sounds • Recognizing 50 sight words • Reading simple text • Using sentence context and pictures or word recognition cues to decode
3 Fledgling Reader	Early/Mid First Grade	• Confirms with beginning and ending consonant sounds • Recognizes 50+ sight words • Reads simple text	• Recognizing and using word families in reading and writing • Recognizing 100+ sight words • Reading more complex text • Developing fluency • Developing comprehension strategies • Self-correcting errors
4 Transitional Reader	Mid/Late First Grade	• Recognizes word families in isolation and in texts • Recognizes 100+ sight words • Reads developed text	• Using word patterns in reading and writing • Developing independent reading using decoding and comprehension strategies • Developing fluency
5 Independent Reader	Early/Late Second Grade	• Reads and writes independently • Uses strategies to figure out new words • Reads fluently • Uses word patterns in reading and writing	• Developing diverse comprehension strategies • Using complex word patterns • Developing fluency in a variety of texts • Responding to text in a variety of ways

> The famous pendulum of educational innovation swings more widely on reading than in any other subject. Pendulum swings of this kind are characteristic of fields driven by fashion, not evidence. Hemlines go up and down because of changing tastes, not new evidence; progress in medicine, engineering, and agriculture, based to a far degree on evidence from rigorous research, is both faster and less subject to radical shifts. In the same way, educational practice must come to be based on evidence—not ideology. (Learning First Alliance, 1998, p. 18)

Typically, when a particular strategy or approach in reading fails to teach some children how to read, educators respond by changing instructional approaches. Unfortunately, the new approach may prove to be effective with only a portion of students, and educators scurry back to the first approach.

Few educators would argue that good reading instruction includes a combination of strategies to teach all children to read. A differentiated approach that includes the best research practices will more likely meet a much wider range of learners (Clay, 1979; Juel, 1988; Stanovich, 1986). The Small-Group Differentiated Reading Model attempts to capture the best practices in reading instruction for beginning readers through the integration of carefully differentiated instructional strategies in each lesson. Rather than relying on one approach or another, each strategy has been carefully weighed in relation to research and its importance to the reading process. Although chapter 3 will address the specific research that supports these lesson strategies, it is important to discuss the developmental process on which each strategy builds.

Rereading

Reading and rereading books are consistent strategies in each stage of the Small-Group Differentiated Reading Model. Beginning readers can become disillusioned with the reading process if they do not actually have a book in their hands and are therefore given books to read in the first stage. Stage 1 begins with books using repetitive text and pictures to tell the story, also known as high picture support. The focus of these strategies in Stage 1 is to have extended practice in tracking print and using picture clues. Stage 2 builds on this process by advancing to text that is less repetitive and has more words on a page. By this time, students are also practicing their decoding skills, which include the knowledge of using beginning and ending sounds and recognizing some sight words. In Stage 3, the emphasis on decoding gradually merges with a stronger focus on comprehension in more complex texts. The need for rereading in each subsequent stage now focuses on the development of fluency. Stage 4 encourages readers to orchestrate decoding and comprehension strategies as students read from a variety of genres. Stage 5 marks a milestone in the reading process in which students have developed the decoding skills and contextual knowledge necessary to become independent readers. The lesson plan in Stage 5 refocuses to encourage longer text selections, the development and the introduction of more complex questioning, and the incorporation of diverse comprehension strategies. The Small-Group Differentiated Reading Model begins with level 1 (Reading Recovery) books in Stage 1 and progresses to level 20 (considered to be a solid second-grade reading level) books in Stage 5.

Word Bank

Whereas sight words are most often taught in the classroom using word walls, this customized word bank is used as a vehicle to increase automaticity in sight word recognition in Stages 1, 2, and 3 of the Small-Group Differentiated Reading Model. Word bank in Stage 1 begins by building a bank of sight words that most members of the reading group recognize automatically. These words are identified in the books being read and reread in the small group to establish a connection between the word bank and the words seen in text. This word bank grows gradually and is reviewed in each lesson to enhance automaticity in word recognition. Approximately 10 words should be mastered during Stage 1. Stage 2 simply continues the process as the teacher works to identify new words to add to the bank. The goal in Stage 2 is to recognize at least 50 sight words. In Stage 3, additional words may be selected from the word study to include in word bank. When the group reaches a goal of recognizing at least 100 sight words, the focus changes.

In Stages 4 and 5, word bank is used for vocabulary development as students begin to read across a variety of genres. Word bank also may be used at this point to house difficult words that are missed routinely in the group. The word bank is differentiated to meet the needs of students as they progress through the stages of beginning reading.

Word Study

As previously noted, word study is traditionally taught in a whole-group setting with little regard for a student's individual readiness level. The word study taught in whole group may or may not be meaningful for individual young readers, depending on their stage of reading development. It is difficult for a student to bring meaning to a lesson on long vowel patterns if he or she lacks the basic knowledge of short vowel sounds or even beginning and ending consonant sounds. Systematic word study provides a safety net for students who fail to glean this knowledge in whole-class lessons and provides confidence for the teacher, who knows that major gaps in word study are not neglected. Just as students are grouped for guided reading based on similar reading processes, basic word study skills also must be considered.

Beginning in Stage 1 with alphabet recognition and production, students advance through systematic phonics instruction that is appropriate to the group's reading level. Stage 2 readers develop phonological awareness of beginning and ending sounds. Beginning in Stage 3, word study advances to a systematic study of short-vowel word families. As part of word study, spelling also is incorporated as a differentiated activity based on the group's current word study focus. Stages 4 and 5 focus on the automatic recognition of common vowel patterns, which completes the word study sequence. Careful pacing through the word study progression is essential. Unlike whole-class phonics instruction, students are encouraged to master basic phonics skills before progressing to the next stage. Differentiation in word study provides a strong backdrop for establishing important decoding skills.

Writing

A developmental writing component in each lesson brings together the target word study strategies in the context of a writing experience. This component allows students to practice known strategies as they relate to writing in a teacher-supported environment. The writing process in the Small-Group Differentiated Reading Model begins in Stage 1 with a shared writing activity. In this shared writing experience, the teacher acts as a scribe while the students contribute to writing a sentence. In an attempt to align the writing experience with the group word study focus, alphabet recognition is emphasized. Standard conventions of print such as capital letters, punctuation, and spacing between words also are demonstrated. After the sentence is completed, the words in the sentence are cut apart and the students are asked to reassemble the sentence. This activity helps students understand the concept of word and sentence construction. In Stage 2, the shared sentence model continues with a shift in focus to attending to beginning and ending consonant sounds that reflect the group's current word study focus. The teacher also uses some familiar words from the group's word bank as part of the sentence structure. This allows the students to see these words as a part of meaningful text. Stage 3 refocuses the writing activity to allow students to write independently as the teacher dictates the sentence. At this point, students are expected to write a complete sentence using correct capitalization, punctuation, and spelling. Stages 4 and 5 require students to write dictated sentences that use variant vowel patterns that are the current focus of word study. This writing activity is usually quick, as students have mastered the required skills to write these simple sentences correctly. Differentiating this writing strategy supports students in their developing reading and writing independence.

New Read

The new read allows students to read a new book daily as they apply known strategies to new text challenges. Extended practice in reading instructionally appropriate books enhances literacy development. In Stage 1, the emergent readers echo read, or read after the teacher has first read the text as the teacher calls attention to the pictures that support the reading. Students develop concept of word in this process and learn to use picture clues as a decoding strategy. In each stage, the teacher also may use the new read as an opportunity to find words for the group word bank. Less echo reading is used in Stage 2 as students focus on beginning sounds and word bank words as decoding strategies. The picture walk introduces the book as the teacher and the students look at the book together and talk about the story based on the pictures. The picture walk is instrumental to reading success for these beginning readers. Stage 3 encourages students to read the new book with strategic support by the teacher. Word bank words (high-frequency words) and word family knowledge support the reading of the new text. The new read in Stages 4 and 5 allows students to orchestrate decoding and comprehension strategies as they move toward reading independence.

What Makes the Small-Group Differentiated Reading Model Successful?

Models are representations that combine common parts into a whole. Models also suggest how the valued parts of a system might work together. Developing a model inclusive of differentiated reading stages and research-based strategies helps us to understand the reading process as a whole. Anchored in research, the Small-Group Differentiated Reading Model brings together many complex reading strategies. However, it is because the model has been systematically developed that the instructional components carry special weight. There are several aspects of this differentiated reading model that support its success.

- Small-group differentiated instruction provides systematic and comprehensive coverage of the strategies required to move students to greater achievement in reading.
- The teacher ensures that the reading activities are "respectful." Every group of students is given quality reading instruction and tasks that are worthwhile, valuable, and matched to students' instructional level.
- Assessment is ongoing and directly linked to instruction. Teachers gather information from both formal and informal assessments about how their students are progressing in their learning at any given point. Whatever the teacher can glean about student reading readiness helps the teacher plan the next steps in reading instruction.
- Students are constantly evaluated and shuffled and reshuffled in flexible groups to best meet instructional needs.
- Small-group differentiated reading provides intensive and continually adjusted instruction in reading, word study, and writing.
- Differentiated reading takes into consideration the individual characteristics of the children, capitalizes on the strengths they have, and expands and challenges their abilities.
- The individual components of the Small-Group Differentiated Reading Model work interactively, building on and supporting one another. Each lesson introduces a new book. The rereading of this book builds sight vocabulary, promotes strategy use, and increases fluency. Additionally, new words for the word bank are selected from the reread selections. The sentence writing includes words taken from the word bank as well as from the word study. Therefore, this model allows for the interactive development of reading, word study, and writing.

Small-Group Differentiated Reading in Balanced Literacy Instruction

Although this book focuses on small-group differentiated reading instruction and its importance, the additional components of a balanced literacy program cannot be overlooked (see Figure 4). Small-group differentiated reading is a critical part of balanced literacy instruction, which, when implemented effectively, gives every student the opportunity to become a successful reader.

FIGURE 4
Balanced Literacy Instruction for Beginning and Struggling Readers

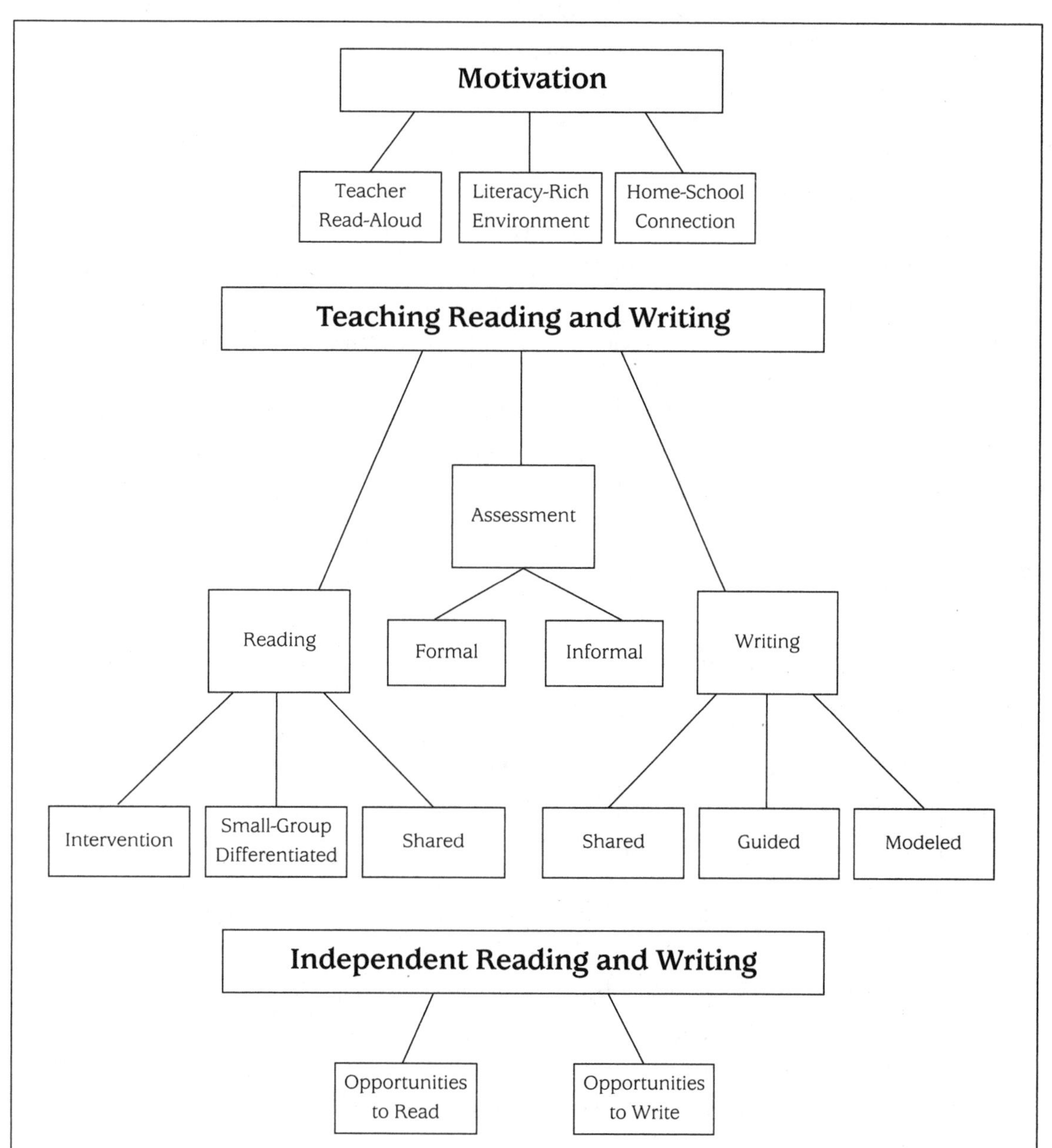

Motivation

Motivation is essential if children are to become successful readers, and it is perhaps the easiest component to implement in the early elementary grades. Children come to school expecting to learn to read. It is only when the system fails to make this a reality that motivation becomes an issue. Reading to children is the ultimate motivator. Reading aloud allows children to connect to the text and experience the excitement and pleasure in reading. My first motivation to become a reader occurred when my fourth-grade teacher, Ms. Bolick, read part of a book to our class and, at the peak of excitement, told us that the book was in the library if we wanted to read it. Ms. Bolick knew how to select the right book to motivate fourth graders. Additionally, teacher read-aloud is a powerful tool for teaching comprehension strategies to children who are beginning the reading process. Pre- and postreading discussions and questions promote student interaction with the text. It is difficult to imagine a motivating environment without books and additional print. Students get excited about reading when they are surrounded by a variety of books to explore, read, and enjoy. It is, therefore, the teacher's responsibility to provide a literacy-rich environment. This affords children many opportunities to listen to and read printed language.

The importance of family support cannot be underestimated in motivating readers. Encouraging literacy in the home supports the total reading process. One powerful way to build the home-school connection is to implement a take-home book program in which students and parents build strong literacy bonds as they read together. Although family support is a plus, the lack of family support cannot be used as an excuse for children who are unable to read. Teachers have more than enough class time with students to motivate and teach them to read.

Teaching Reading and Writing

The centerpiece of a balanced literacy program lies in the teaching of reading and writing. This is what I refer to as direct, face-to-face teaching. Some whole language advocates once thought that if you immersed children in reading and writing, they would somehow learn these skills on their own. Educators now realize that this is not true for many students. The *teaching* of reading and writing is essential to increasing student achievement. As teachers, we probably do a better job with shared reading than with any other component in balanced literacy instruction. The use of Big Books has been instrumental in promoting whole-group shared reading over the past two decades. The challenge appears to be in equipping teachers with the skills necessary to become effective in small-group reading situations. My motivation in writing this book is my belief that many teachers lack this expertise. Although typically not included, reading intervention is a part of balanced literacy instruction as it relates to beginning and struggling readers. No matter how hard we try, we realize that some children need additional one-on-one assistance. We also know that to be successful, this intervention must be early and intensive.

Assessment goes hand in hand with quality reading and writing instruction. Assessment provides teachers with important information that will guide the reading and writing processes and has particular implications for small-group reading instruction. Assessment will, in fact, assist the teacher in making critical decisions concerning placement and pacing in small-group instruction. Assessment should provide the teacher with a road map for the successful teaching of reading and writing. Both formal and informal assessments can provide important feedback to teachers. Used effectively, this information is instrumental in making curricular decisions that increase literacy learning.

The writing process develops in predictable stages, as does the reading process. Writing is a skill that must be modeled, supported, and practiced. Writing and reading develop together and are therefore taught most successfully as integrated processes. For this reason, writing is included as a part of the small-group reading model presented in this book.

Independent Reading and Writing

Finally, "practice makes perfect" is a phrase that we need to pay closer attention to as teachers. Students get better at reading and writing by practicing these skills at appropriate independent levels. This is the piece of the balanced reading program that can take place while small-group reading groups are being conducted. The biggest mistake made during small-group reading is assigning tasks to the rest of the class that are not at appropriate independent reading or writing levels. Students become frustrated, management problems surface, and off-task behavior is exhibited. Careful planning for independent reading and writing activities promotes quality time spent away from the direct supervision of the teacher.

A Look Ahead

Chapter 2 discusses the two assessment components that support the Small-Group Differentiated Reading Model: the Early Reading Screening Instrument (ERSI) and the Reading Review. These assessments provide valuable information for curriculum planning and individual assessment. Using information gained through the ERSI allows teachers to make informed decisions as they assign students for small-group instruction based on individual literacy needs. As literacy levels increase, the Reading Review is useful as teachers continue to track student progress, determine fluency rates, and assign appropriate texts to maximize learning opportunities.

Chapter 3 begins with an in-depth look at the individual strategies of the Small-Group Differentiated Reading Model, along with the research that supports them. These components include rereading, word bank, word study, writing, and the new read. The last part of chapter 3 addresses the issue of how to effectively engage the rest of the class during small-group reading instruction. Suggestions for implementing literacy centers, whole-class activities, and follow-up exercises to small-group reading also are discussed. Finally, classroom management and organizational alternatives are explored.

Chapters 4 through 8 are structured similarly and present the five stages of early reading development. In each chapter, a brief review of student characteristics associated with each specific reading stage is presented followed by appropriate text recommendations. A lesson plan that supports each developmental stage also is included in each of these chapters. Step-by-step directions are given for lesson plan implementation, followed by selected classroom dialogue. Where appropriate, Literacy Center Alerts are included as suggestions for easy-to-implement activities.

The appendixes contain essential information concerning assessment and the materials necessary to implement the Small-Group Differentiated Reading Model. Appendix A includes the abbreviated teacher directions for administering the ERSI along with the individual score sheets. Additionally, the testing components are available as blackline masters. Appendix B contains the word study materials, including letter cards, picture cards, and word study cards. Appendix C provides the materials needed for the word scramble and writing activities. The cut-up sentences used in Stage 2 as well as suggested dictated sentences for Stages 3, 4, and 5 are located here. Appendix D holds a variety of auxiliary materials that can be used to support the model.

CHAPTER 2

Planning for Instruction and Assessing Student Progress in the Small-Group Differentiated Reading Model

An ongoing system of assessment is critical to teaching beginning reading. Prior to beginning small-group differentiated reading instruction, it is essential to assess the literacy knowledge of each student. The Early Reading Screening Instrument (ERSI), developed by Darrell Morris (1998), provides reliable and essential information about students' print-related knowledge. The teacher uses this information as a guide for forming groups and tracking progress in small-group instruction. Several parts of the ERSI can be readministered to determine gains. This is particularly useful for emergent and beginning readers.

After initial reading groups are established, the Reading Review will assess students' reading and fluency levels as they progress through the five stages of beginning reading. This ongoing assessment will provide valuable information to teachers as they group and regroup students to best meet students' instructional needs. Planning for instruction will be critical to each student's success.

Early Reading Screening Instrument

Several research studies verify the effectiveness of the ERSI. In a study conducted by Lombardino, Defillipo, Sarisky, and Montgomery (1992), the predictive validity of the ERSI was verified. The researchers found that the ERSI, when given to kindergarten students near the end of the year, correlated .73 with the Woodcock-Johnson Comprehension Subtest administered to the same students at the end of first grade. Other studies in North Carolina reached similar conclusions. For example, in a rural county, student performance on the ERSI at the beginning of first grade correlated .70 with their passage-reading ability at the end of first grade (Perney, Morris, & Carter, 1997).

The ERSI is administered on an individual basis and takes about 20 minutes to complete and evaluate the results. This assessment looks at the basic skills that researchers (e.g., Chall, 1987; Dowhower, 1987; Reitsma, 1988) believe are critical to early reading success. These areas include the following:

- Alphabet recognition and production—Does the student recognize both upper- and lowercase letters? Can the student reproduce letters in random order?

- Concept of word—Can the student track print? Does he or she understand what a word is and that words make up our language?
- Sight words—Does the student recognize some basic sight words in isolation?
- Phoneme awareness—Does the student hear individual sounds in words? How does this relate to his or her development in spelling?
- Decodable words—Can the student decode simple unknown words using phonics knowledge?

Although the ERSI is effective in determining students' knowledge of printed words, perhaps the most important assessment as it relates to the ongoing reading process is the Reading Review, which accurately determines instructional reading and fluency levels for students. The Reading Review is a brief assessment used as a student reads 100 words in a new book. As the child reads, the teacher simply records errors made by the student. The teacher then uses this information to determine if the level is too easy, too difficult, or at the correct instructional level. Fluency rates are strong indicators for student progress toward independence. The Reading Review is appropriate to use beginning with Stage 3.

Administration of the Early Reading Screening Instrument

This section gives step-by-step directions on how to administer the ERSI. The individual student test and abbreviated teacher directions are found in Appendix A.

1.1 Alphabet

Section 1.1 of the test evaluates the student's knowledge of the alphabet and production of letters. Many students come to school able to identify and reproduce many of the letters of the alphabet, but others may lack these skills and require further instruction. Not every student needs to review every letter. Assessment will reveal to the teacher who needs extensive help learning the alphabet.

Alphabet Recognition

Procedure: Using a random list of upper- and lowercase letters such as the one below, ask the student to name the letters as you point to them:

A F K P W Z	a f k p w z
B H O J U	b h o j u
C Y L Q M	c y l q m
D N S X I	d n s x i
E G R V T	e g r v t

Scoring: Using the Individual Score Sheet, Section 1.1 (see Appendix A, p. 128), record the information noting errors and no-attempts for each letter. If the student is unable to recognize the letter, simply circle the letter to note nonrecognition. If the student gives the incorrect letter response, write the incorrect letter above the letter. It is important to note that reversals are counted as errors, but self-corrects are counted as correct and are indicated with a check (✓) beside the first incorrect response. Record the number of correctly identified upper- (0–26) and lowercase (0–26) letters.

Alphabet Production

This task is more advanced than alphabet recognition. The student will complete this section of the test on the lined form provided in Appendix A (see p. 131).

Procedure: Begin by telling the student to write either an upper- or lowercase letter (not both). Using the order of the alphabet in the previous alphabet recognition section, call out the letters in random order. If the student is unable to write a letter, record that information on Section 1.1 of the Individual Score Sheet. The following shows a student alphabet production assessment that reflects two errors.

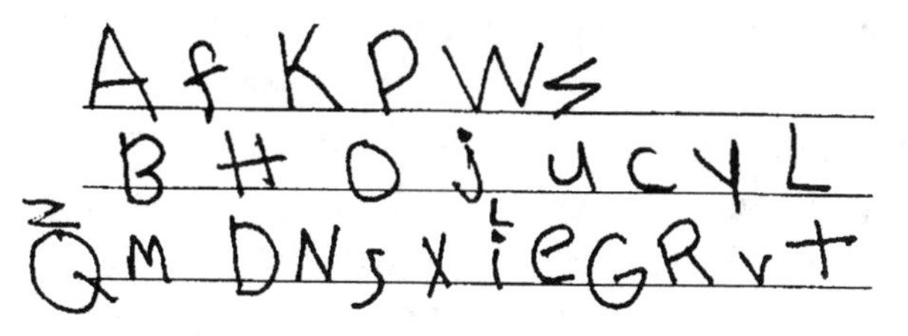

Scoring: Count each correctly produced letter. In this subtest, reversals (such as *b-d*) are counted as correct (unlike the recognition section). However, upside down reversals (such as *p-d*) are counted as incorrect.

To obtain the Alphabet subtest score, add the scores from each section together:

Recognition Upper (0–26) (a)
Recognition Lower (0–26) (b)
Reproduction (0–26) (c)

The top score, if there were no errors, would total 78. Write these scores in the scoring section at the top of the Individual Score Sheet.

Upper (26)		Lower (26)		Prod. (26)		Total (78)
(a)	+	(b)	+	(c)	=	

1.2 Concept of Word (The Katie Book)

Concept of word refers to the beginning reader's ability to match spoken words with written words when he or she reads a line of text. This important concept is often overlooked in early reading assessments. However, before a student is able to read, he or she must first be able to track print. In other words, after the teacher models finger-point reading a sentence, the student should be able to accurately finger point to each word as he or she recites the sentence. This does not mean that students are being asked to actually read the words in the sentence. The evaluator is simply trying to determine if the student recognizes that individual words make up a sentence. Until a student can repeat and point to the words in a sentence, he or she will have difficulty learning sight words or developing the strategy of using letter sounds to decode words in text (Clay, 1979; Morris, 1993).

There are two ERSI subtests that evaluate a student's concept of word (1.2 and 2.1). These two subtests are not given in sequence. Instead, Test 1.3, Word Recognition, comes between the two subtests. To make this sequence easier to follow, the two concept of word subtests are discussed together because they are eventually scored as one test.

The Katie Book subtest requires the student to finger-point read three different sentences and identify preselected target words within the sentences. The three pages of the book will be covered and stapled together to make a book (see Appendix A, p. 123).

Procedure: Begin by asking the student what he or she thinks is happening in the picture. Tell the student (while pointing to the picture) that the sentence tells us what is happening. Ask the student to watch as you read and point to each word. (Read and finger point the sentence one time.) Then, ask the student to read and finger point the sentence by himself or herself. After completing the sentence, quickly point to the first target word (on the first page, the word is *walking*) and ask, "Can you read this word?" Move to the second target word, *rain*, and repeat the question. Use this same procedure on pages 2 and 3 of the Katie Book.

Scoring: The student receives two scores—one for reading and finger pointing and another for reading the underlined words. The score sheet should be filled in as each sentence is completed. Finger pointing is scored as either correct (✓) or incorrect (**0**). If the student correctly finger points **each** word in the sentence, she or he receives one point (✓). If there is even one mistake in pointing or calling a word incorrectly, the student receives no points (**0**). Figure 5 represents the score box for the Katie Book. The student scored 2 points on pointing and 3 points on identifying words.

Be consistent in your scoring procedures to get the most accurate information. There are 3 possible points for pointing and 6 possible points for words.

FIGURE 5
Katie Book Score Sheet

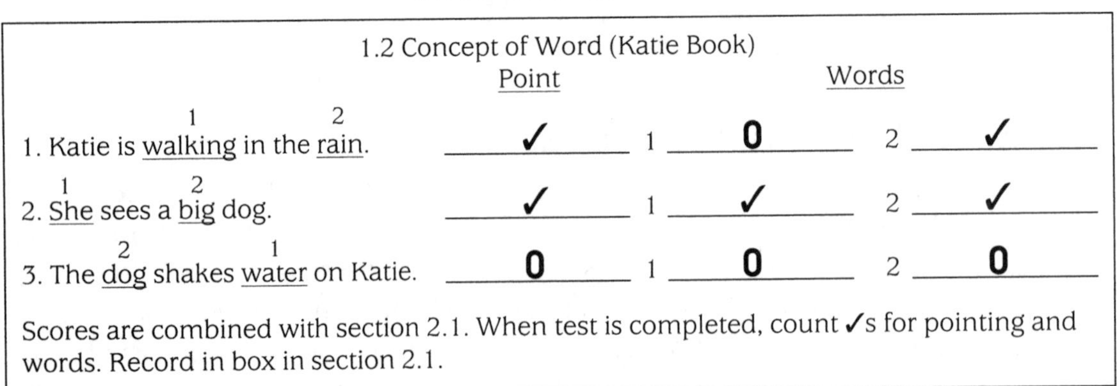

1.2 Concept of Word (Katie Book)

	Point		Words		
1. Katie is walking[1] in the rain[2].	✓	1	**0**	2	✓
2. She[1] sees a big[2] dog.	✓	1	✓	2	✓
3. The dog[2] shakes water[1] on Katie.	**0**	1	**0**	2	**0**

Scores are combined with section 2.1. When test is completed, count ✓s for pointing and words. Record in box in section 2.1.

Reprinted from Morris, D. (1998). Assessing printed word knowledge in beginning readers: The Early Reading Screening Instrument (ERSI). *Illinois Reading Council Journal, 26*(2), 30–40.

2.1 Concept of Word (*My Home*)

Procedure: Begin this subtest by sharing the cover of the book *My Home* (Melser, 1998) with the student (see Appendix A, page 125). Discuss the cover and look at each picture in the book and have the student identify the animals before beginning the test.

Then, turn back to the first page and begin reading the book. Ask the student to watch as you read the first sentence (point to each word). Then, ask the student to finger-point read. Record the student's performance on the answer sheet (**0** or ✓). When you begin on page 3, ask the student to read the final three pages by himself or herself. (There should be no more assistance or modeling.) If the student cannot continue, model and finger point the sentences. (No points should be given, though.) Word identification occurs only on the first two pages. Figure 6 shows one student's assessment using *My Home*. The student scored 4 points for correctly finger pointing and 2 points for correct word identification.

FIGURE 6
***My Home* Score Sheet**

2.1 Concept of Word (*My Home*)

Page		Point	Word
(2)	"My home is here," said the bird.	✓	✓
(3)	"My home is here," said the frog.	✓	0
(4)	"My home is here," said the pig.	✓	
(5)	"My home is here," said the dog.	0	
(7)	"My home is here," said the rabbit.	✓	

Note: Count ✓s for pointing and words from sections 1.2 and 2.1 and record totals below.
CORRECT (point) 6 /8 (d)
Katie Book and *My Home*
CORRECT (word) 5 /8 (e)
Katie Book and *My Home*

Reprinted from Morris, D. (1998). Assessing printed word knowledge in beginning readers: The Early Reading Screening Instrument (ERSI). *Illinois Reading Council Journal, 26*(2), 30–40.

Scoring: This score will be combined with the score on the Katie Book for a total score. Transfer the combined scores for pointing in the Katie Book and *My Home* to the point box (d). Do the same for both books in the word box (e). There are 16 total possible points.

Concept of Word		
Point (8)	Word (8)	Total (16)
______ (d)	______ (e)	______

2.2 Phoneme Awareness (Spelling)

It might seem to some educators that spelling is an inappropriate way to assess early reading ability. There are, however, research-based reasons for doing so. First, a student's spelling and reading ability are highly correlated in the early primary grades (K–2). Morris and Perney (1984) report a .82 correlation between first graders' January spelling ability and their May, end-of-year, word-recognition ability. Second, and more important, spelling gives us insight into a student's ability to read words by looking at how he or she spells words. This is because an abstract, developing word knowledge underlies the ability to both read and spell (Gill, 1992; Henderson, 1990). This subtest will help determine exactly where a student should begin in a program of word study.

Procedure: This assessment is a 12-word spelling task in which students write the sounds they hear in words. This subtest begins with the examiner modeling a "sound-it-out" spelling of two sample words, *mat* and *lip*. Tell the student that you are going to write the word *mat*. Ask the student which letter you should write down first. (Praise a correct response. If an incorrect response or no response is given, still write the *m* on the paper and say that the first letter is *m*.) Ask the student which letter you should write down next. Complete the first word. Continue on to the next sample word, *lip*.

After demonstrating the two examples, give the student the pencil and designated answer sheet (see Appendix A, p. 131). Tell the student that he or she is going to write some words. Read the words on the list (you may use the word in a sentence, if necessary). Prompts may be used only on the first and second words (e.g., What sound do you hear next?). No prompts should be given on the remaining words. Remind the student to write every sound that he or she hears in the word. The purpose of this exercise is not to frustrate children but to get diagnostic information. If the student fails to give at least the initial sound of both the sample words and each of the first two test words, stop the test.

Scoring: Scoring involves counting the number of phonemes (sounds) in each word the student writes. Six words in the test contain three phonemes (*back*, *feet*, *mail*, *side*, *chin*, and *road*), and the other six words have four phonemes (*step*, *junk*, *picking*, *dress*, *peeked*, and *lamp*). The following shows one student's responses to the phoneme awareness (spelling) subtest along with the points given for each response.

1.	Bak	3
2.	fet	3
3.	sP	2
4.	JK	2
5.	peckN	4
6.	ML	2
7.	SID	3
8.	JN	2
9.	JES	3
10.	PET	3
11.	LAP	3
12.	WOD	3

A scoring guide will help you determine the number of points to credit to each word (see Appendix A, p. 119).

1.3 Word Recognition (Basal Words)

Word recognition is central in learning to read. Beginning first-grade students should be able to recognize at least a few common sight words. Students who have some basic sight-word knowledge have an advantage over students who do not recognize any words.

There are two parts in the word recognition test. This first assessment is a common list of sight words, and the assessment that follows in the next section contains a set of decodable words.

Procedure: Begin by telling the student that he or she will be reading a list of words. Reassure the student that you do not expect him or her to know all the words.

is, come, good, here, like, and, other, make, work, day

Point to the words, one word at a time, and ask the student to read them. Record any attempts, especially if he or she is sounding out the word. A student who calls *like, lake* is much more advanced than a student who calls *like, tree*.

Scoring: Simply count the number of words correctly identified by the student and enter the number in the score box.

2.3 Word Recognition (Decodable Words)

Procedure: Follow the same procedure for this list of words as was done with the basal words. The words in this list follow a consonant-vowel-consonant pattern that gives students the ability to use phonics or sound-it-out strategies. Again, record any attempts the student makes.

cap, net, win, bug, fat, mop, led, dig, job, mud

Scoring: Score each subtest (1.3 and 2.3) separately. There are 10 points possible for each test. The student gets one point for each word that is pronounced correctly. Although an attempt does not count as a correct score, the recorded information does provide important diagnostic information.

Calculating the ERSI Score

Use the following formulas to calculate the total score. The formula converts the subtest scores to 40 total points. Transfer the scores to the formulas, calculate them, and then add the four scores together for the grand total (round to the nearest 10th; .05 rounds up).

$$\text{Alphabet Knowledge } \frac{(a + b + c)}{78} \times 10 = \text{Total}$$

$$\text{Concept of Word } \frac{(d + e)}{16} \times 10 = \text{Total}$$

$$\text{Phoneme Awareness } \frac{(f)}{42} \times 10 = \text{Total}$$

$$\text{Word Recognition } \frac{(g + h)}{20} \times 10 = \text{Total}$$

Alphabet Knowledge				Concept of Word			Phoneme Awareness		Word Recognition			
Upper	Lower	Prod.	Total	Point	Word	Total	Count	Total	Basal	Dec.	Total	Grand Total
26	26	26		8	8		42		10	10		
___	___	___	___	___	___	___	___	___	___	___	___	___
(a)	(b)	(c)		(d)	(e)		(f)		(g)	(h)		

Table 1 shows how an entire first-grade class's performance on the ERSI can be summarized on one page.

TABLE 1
Class Tally on the Early Reading Screening Instrument

	Alphabet Knowledge				Concept of Word			Phoneme Awareness		Word Recognition			
Name	**Upper**	**Lower**	**Prod.**	**Total**	**Point**	**Word**	**Total**	**Count**	**Total**	**Basal**	**Dec.**	**Total**	**Grand Total**
Jennifer	26	26	26	10	8	8	10	42	10	9	10	9.5	39.5
Susan	25	23	26	9.5	8	8	10	37	8.8	3	2	5.0	33.3
Harrison	26	25	26	9.9	8	8	10	35	8.3	2	3	2.5	30.7
Leslie	26	25	26	9.9	8	8	10	31	7.4	1	3	2.0	29.3
Paul	26	24	24	9.5	8	7	9.4	35	8.3	1	3	2.0	29.2
Gloria	26	24	24	9.5	7	6	8.1	31	7.4	1	1	1.0	26.0
Katherine	24	24	24	9.2	7	3	6.3	25	6.0	1	1	1.0	22.5
Patrick	26	22	24	9.2	7	3	6.3	21	5.0	1	1	1.0	21.5
Derrick	25	23	26	9.5	7	3	6.3	16	3.8	0	0	0	19.6
Jill	26	21	22	8.8	7	4	6.9	14	3.3	0	0	0	19.0
Nick	26	24	24	9.5	6	1	4.4	14	3.3	1	1	1.0	18.2
Beth	25	22	24	9.1	2	2	2.5	21	5.0	0	1	.5	17.1
Dee	12	8	6	3.3	2	3	3.1	12	2.9	1	1	1.0	10.3
Clint	16	8	10	4.4	3	3	3.8	8	1.9	0	0	0	10.1
Mary	14	10	12	4.6	3	3	3.8	5	1.2	0	0	0	9.6
Debbie	12	8	6.0	3.3	1	1	1.3	14	3.3	0	0	0	7.9
Polly	8	2	3	1.6	5	2	4.4	0	0	0	0	0	6.0
Helen	10	5	6	2.7	1	1	1.3	5	1.2	0	0	0	5.2

Implications for Instruction

The ERSI provides an individual profile of each student's literacy knowledge. The teacher learns which students lack foundational alphabet knowledge or concept of word. The spelling assessment is essential in determining where students should begin in word study. For example, students who know their letters and can represent most initial and final consonants are ready for word families. This assessment also identifies students who already are reading some sight words; these students can be assigned to appropriately challenging materials. Students who achieve a total score of 20 or below often need an intensive one-on-one reading intervention program, along with appropriate classroom reading instruction.

Forming Initial Reading Groups

Based on the data gathered from the ERSI, preliminary groupings and instructional decisions can be made. The beginning first-grade class list shown in Table 1 will be used as a basis for discussion. In examining the class chart, divide the group into thirds. If the class is larger, consider four groups that will meet alternately. Realistically, no more than three reading instructional groups can be successfully taught daily. The six students scoring 26 and above possess many of the essential skills for becoming successful readers. They have alphabet knowledge, are able to track print, can represent beginning and ending consonant sounds, and even know some words. Based on this information, these students would be ready for Stage 3 (see Figure 3 on page 8).

The students who fall within the midrange between 17.1 and 22.5 recognize and produce most of the alphabet but need more work in tracking print, understanding concept of word, and identifying beginning and ending consonant sounds. These students should begin in Stage 2.

The students in the lower third of the class need immediate, intensive assistance in both small-group and one-on-one instruction. The students should begin in Stage 1 and focus on concept of word and alphabet recognition. These students should progress quickly to Stage 2 and begin consonant-sound discrimination. Without a strong instructional plan, these students will quickly become at risk for serious reading difficulties.

Grouping students based on information gained from the ERSI provides a basis to make sound instructional decisions. It is imperative that no reading group remains static. Students progress at various rates and must be constantly observed and assessed for regrouping. Shifting students among groups allows each student to be appropriately challenged and always on the instructional edge.

Planning for Larger Class Sizes

Realistically, many classes average 24 or more students; therefore, reading groups cannot meet daily. Be creative in how the students' needs can be best met. Lower-level students should be seen more frequently. Plan your weekly schedule to include an extra reading group on days that have fewer extra activities, such as music or library.

The following schedule, for four reading groups, allows the lowest two groups (A and B) to be seen four times weekly. The two higher groups are seen three times a week. On Thursday, two special classes (music and gym) reduce the time available for three groups.

Monday	A	B	C
Tuesday	A	B	C
Wednesday	A	B	D
Thursday	A	D	
Friday	B	C	D

Another schedule for four reading groups allows two groups to meet per day, with each group meeting for approximately 30 minutes. Although this schedule allows for only minimal reading instruction, some small-group instruction is better than none.

Monday	A	B
Tuesday	C	D
Wednesday	A	B
Thursday	C	D
Friday	A	B

Look for additional assistance with reading groups. Teaching assistants can conduct a reading group by following a structured lesson plan. Title I teachers, inclusion teachers, student teachers, and regular volunteers also have been successful in assisting with this small-group instruction. The more often each group is seen, the more powerful the instructional impact.

Continual Evaluations

Administering portions of the ERSI can give an objective measure of a child's individual growth. Instead of administering these parts of the test individually, the assessment can be done in small groups. For example, by administering the Alphabet Recognition subtest, the teacher can find out exactly which letters still need to be taught.

The spelling assessment also is useful to readminister as a measure of growth. Figure 7 compares Paul's spelling performance at the beginning of the school year with his performance at the end of the school year.

Pacing

The most important factor that drives student reading achievement is appropriate instructional pacing. In other words, are students moving too quickly or too slowly within a reading group? My experience has been that as cautious, conscientious teachers

FIGURE 7
Comparison of Paul's Results on the Phoneme Awareness (Spelling) Subtest

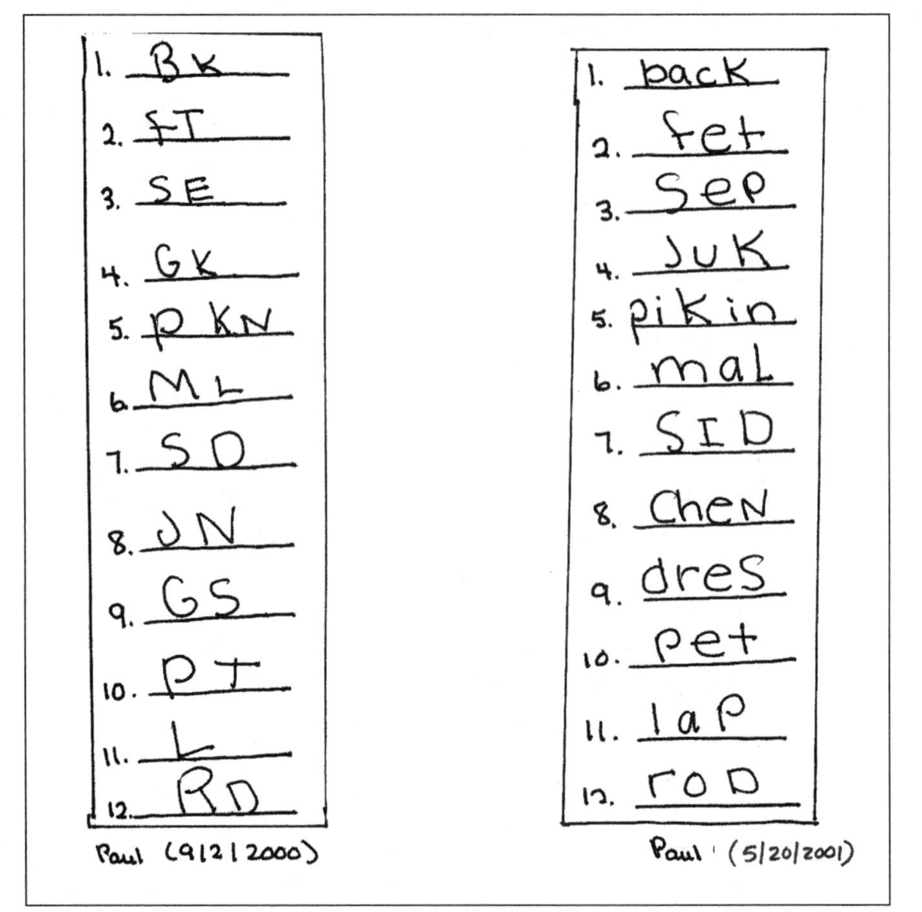

we tend to err on the side of moving students too slowly. We want to make sure that they have truly mastered the material. Most students don't have time to repeat what they already know in their reading lesson; this should be left to independent practice. A good rule of thumb is to do what is instructionally challenging yet achievable for the group. The Reading Review, which is discussed in the next section, is one way to assist in determining appropriate pacing.

The Reading Review

Although running records are important in diagnosing particular strengths and weaknesses in readers, a complete running record may not be necessary to determine when to move a group to the next reading level. A simplified version of the traditional running record model, the Reading Review, serves this purpose as well as acting as an oral reading fluency measure.

Procedure for Determining Instructional Level

The instructional level is the highest level at which a student can read successfully with supervision and support by the teacher. Children learn best when they receive help from experts on tasks that would be too difficult for them to accomplish on their own (Vygotsky, 1934/1978). The Reading Review (see score sheet in Figure 8) is a quick assessment that can be completed with relative ease, allowing teachers many more chances to record children's oral reading than if they were completing a more complex running record.

FIGURE 8
Reading Review Score Sheet

Name ______________________ Date ____________

Recorder ______________________ Classroom Teacher ____________

Highest Level at 90–94% Accuracy

Instructional Level ____________

Fluency Rate ____________

Page	Title Total Words ________	Errors Per Page
	Total Errors	

ACCURACY FORMULA

$$\frac{\text{Running Words} - \text{Errors}}{\text{Running Words}} \times 100 = \_\_\_\_\_\_ \text{ \% accuracy}$$

Reading Fluency Rate
Number of words read correctly in one minute = fluency rate

Begin by selecting a book that the student has never read before as a basis for the assessment, and mark a one hundred word passage. (Do not include words on the cover or title page.) For early readers, a picture walk of the book is appropriate. More advanced readers should be given only the title and a brief introduction to the book. Then the student should begin reading the passage. Using the Reading Review score sheet, the teacher simply makes a check whenever the student misses a word. Words that are self-corrected by the student within three seconds are not counted as mistakes. Proper nouns (names, cities, countries, etc.) are counted as incorrect the first time only. If the student skips a line, it is counted as one mistake. If the student does not know a word, wait three seconds and then tell him or her the word and count it as one mistake. When the initial passage is completed, quickly check to determine the percentage of correctly read words, counting 1 point for each mistake. If the student reads with a 95% or above accuracy rate, the book is too easy and a book at the next highest level should be tested. Students reading a passage at 90%–94% accuracy are reading a book at the appropriate instructional level. For students reading below a 90% accuracy rate, complete another Reading Review at the next lowest level until an accuracy rate of between 90% and 94% is reached. Following is the information necessary to determine appropriate instructional levels:

95%–100%	**Independent Level** Move to the next level
90%–94%	**Instructional Level** Remain at present level
Below 90%	**Frustration Level** Move down a level

This assessment also can be used for students reading at a lower level by using 50 words instead of 100. The accuracy rate is determined by counting off 2 points for each mistake. Be sure that the test is administered consistently among readers by following the same procedures for all students for the most reliable information.

Although it may not always be possible to group students based on their exact instructional levels, the Reading Review is useful for group placement. Reading groups should remain flexible as students are routinely assessed and placed in groups that most accurately reflect appropriate instructional levels. Reading Reviews allow teachers to collect dozens of samples of a child's reading as he or she progresses through the year.

Determining Fluency Rate

LaBerge and Samuels (1974) describe the fluent reader as one whose decoding processes are automatic, requiring little conscious attention to word recognition while comprehending text. A student's fluency rate at Stage 3 and above is easy to obtain. (The fluency rate does not need to be determined at Stages 1 and 2 because students in these stages are basically memorizing and finger pointing to simple text.) Using a watch with a second hand, the teacher records the number of words read correctly in one minute. As in determining the instructional level, words self-corrected within three seconds are scored as accurate. Omitted words, substitutions, and hesitations of more than three seconds are counted as errors. The number of words read correctly in one minute is the called *oral fluency rate*.

Determining fluency rates for early readers can be difficult. Sixty words per minute is often cited as an average first-grade rate (see Morris, 1999), but at what point in first grade? Based on my experience, the following benchmarks might be useful for defining appropriate fluency rates for fledgling, transitional, and independent readers.

Stage	**Fluency Rate** (correct words per minute)
3—Fledgling	40
4—Transitional	60
5—Independent	70

Benchmark Books

To complete the Reading Review, a set of benchmarks must be dedicated to the assessment process. Several textbook companies offer sets of these books, or each school or group of teachers can meet and decide books at each level that seem to be the most representative. These benchmark books are used for Reading Reviews for ongoing assessment as well as for assisting in making decisions about when to move individuals or the reading group to the next level. If most students in the group do well with the Reading Review at the current book level, the teacher should be confident about moving to the next level. Conversely, students who do poorly could be shifted to a lower reading group.

Recognizing Reading Levels in Literacy Instruction

The assessment of student reading levels in the Reading Review gives additional information for planning in a balanced literacy program. Although the instructional reading level is optimal for small-group instruction, there also is a place for text that is at an independent reading level or even a frustration reading level.

Reading Level	**Appropriate Place in Balanced Reading Model**
Independent (95%–100% accuracy)	Books to use for independent reading, take-home reading, literacy centers
Instructional (90%–94% accuracy)	Books for use in small-group differentiated reading
Frustration (Below 90%)	Books for shared reading or teacher read-aloud

Independent Level

Daily independent reading is critical to total literacy development. This gives students the opportunity to develop fluency and allows them to experience the sheer pleasure of reading a book independently. As appropriate instructional levels for reading are determined, the appropriate independent levels also are established. If a student is reading at an instructional level 8, books at level 7 or below would be appropriate for independent reading. Reading these books helps students review what they already know. Such reading requires less energy and intensity so that readers become more confident. Additionally, independent reading allows students to focus on the meaning of the text. Although independent reading is important, we also must recognize that this reading by itself will not move the reading process forward. For this to take place, the instructional level must be addressed.

Instructional Level

What happens when students are given books at their instructional level for small-group differentiated reading? With the support of the teacher, it pushes students beyond their current reading level. The difficulty of the text and tasks needs to be beyond the level at which the student is already capable of independent functioning. Reading at the instructional level also allows students to build the use of effective cueing systems: Does it look right, does it sound right, does it make sense? Additionally, students are able to use prior knowledge to solve new challenges. Using appropriate instructional levels in combination with an effective reading model enables readers to strengthen their reading processes.

Frustration Level

Books that are clearly too difficult should never be used in small-group or independent reading situations. Reading books that are too difficult becomes a matter of saying one word after another in a laborious reading of isolated words. Students quickly lose the meaning of the text and become frustrated and dislike reading. These students are unable to use known strategies to become better readers. Additionally, these students may begin to withdraw or misbehave when they lose self-confidence.

Books that cannot be successfully read by students have an important place in balanced literacy instruction. During shared reading and read-aloud, the teacher has an opportunity to share these books with students. Stories rich in content and story structure provide opportunities for development of knowledge and reading comprehension skills. These reading experiences also provide motivation for students as they explore a variety of genres unavailable at their instructional reading level.

Conclusion

The first step in teaching a student to read is to determine what each student can do as a reader. Although beginning readers are generally viewed as a homogeneous group, there are important prerequisites to reading that should be considered individually. The ERSI assesses alphabet knowledge, concept of word, sight word vocabulary, phoneme awareness (spelling), and the ability to decode simple phonemically correct words. The initial assessment data provided by the ERSI serves two major functions. First, it assists teachers in placing students in appropriate instructional groups based on individual strengths and weaknesses. Second, the ERSI provides initial assessment data that can be used as a benchmark against which a student's future progress can be compared.

Although the ERSI provides important initial instructional data, it is only a start. Assessment, to be effective, must be an ongoing process. The Reading Review should be included as an integral part of this reading model. These assessments provide important pacing information that is critical for maximum reading growth. As the stages of reading unfold in the following chapters, the need for ongoing assessment will become clear.

CHAPTER 3

Instructional Strategies in the Small-Group Differentiated Reading Model

The Small-Group Differentiated Reading Model shares some of the same components as Reading Recovery, such as rereading and writing, but correlates more closely with Early Steps because of its systematic word study. The power of this model lies in the strong research base (e.g., Adams, 1990; Morris, 1999; Santa & Hoien, 1999) of its components: rereading, word bank, word study, writing, and the new read.

Carefully devised lesson plans integrate these individual strategies in a supportive and meaningful way. Ideally, a lesson should last no more than 30 minutes and be used with groups of no more than six students. A commitment to seeing each group on a regular basis is essential to the success of the program.

Although specific steps for model implementation will be discussed in chapters 4 through 8, it is important to examine each lesson plan component and the research that supports these literacy strategies.

Rereading

Each small-group reading lesson begins by having students reread previously read books. Depending on the length of the book, this could involve one or two rereads. The book from the previous day becomes the first reread for the next day.

Research is clear about the need to develop fluency in readers through rereading (Samuels, 1979). Fluency is the vehicle that takes the child from focusing on the words to focusing on the meaning of the text. Quite simply, practicing reading makes better, more confident readers. As students reread, they are able to increase their speed, use phrasing techniques, and become more automatic with the reading process. *Automaticity* has become a new buzzword in reading research. It refers to how quickly or automatically students can recognize words so they can focus on the meaning of the text.

Repeated reading is an excellent technique for helping children achieve automaticity in reading. Repeated reading facilitates automatic decoding among average readers and among special populations (Chomsky, 1978; Samuels, 1979). Furthermore, rereading can lead to improved comprehension (Dowhower, 1987; Herman, 1985; Rasinski & Reinking, 1988). Poor readers who engage in repeated readings show marked improvement in speed, accuracy, and expression during oral rereading, and, more important, improvement is noted in reading comprehension. Support for repeated reading also can be found in theories based on information processing paradigms such as Samuels and LaBerge's (1983) automaticity theory and Perfetti and Lesgold's (1979) verbal efficiency model, in which the practice of rereading is seen as increasing the speed of word recognition.

Students need to become fluent or automatic in decoding to become skilled readers. After students have achieved some accuracy in word recognition, additional rereading enables them to become fluent. By exposing students to repeated reading, teachers help students become automatic decoders and thus good readers.

The Importance of Oral Reading

Whereas traditional guided reading models do not encourage individual oral reading by students, the Small-Group Differentiated Reading Model embraces oral reading as an important strategy. The National Reading Panel (National Institute of Child Health and Human Development, 2000) points out that guided oral reading with teacher feedback has a significant positive impact on word recognition, reading fluency, and comprehension. In fact, the report further states that guided oral reading benefits both poor and good readers at least through grade 4. Conversely, the report was unable to determine if silent reading improves fluency. The Small-Group Differentiated Reading Model includes oral reading as students read and reread a variety of texts.

Frequent opportunities to read aloud make sense for beginning readers. First, oral reading helps connect children with experiences they have had at home, preschools, or kindergartens where adults have read to them. In addition, oral reading gives teachers observable characteristics of an otherwise unobservable process. This provides teachers with a means for checking progress, diagnosing problems, and focusing instruction. Ultimately, oral reading serves to provide young readers a way to share their emerging abilities with their peers, parents, and teachers.

Opportunities to read aloud and listen to others read is part of a total literacy community. When teachers read aloud, it whets the appetite of children. Similarly, oral reading, when done appropriately, builds self-confidence and a desire to share good stories with others.

Round-Robin Reading

As with many reading strategies, traditional round-robin reading in which students take turns reading orally has been deemed a poor strategy because of its misuse. This misuse stems from practices that forced students to read instructionally inappropriate text and an unequal distribution of turns. However, this technique has more benefits than downfalls when used appropriately.

Getting the most from the traditional practice of round-robin reading requires that the teacher distribute turns equally among the children in the group, skillfully handle mistakes, and focus attention on meaning. An issue in round-robin reading comes when a teacher always calls on volunteers; the more assertive and confident children get more turns. This is undesirable because research shows that children reading aloud and receiving instruction from the teacher get far more instructional feedback than the students following along (Anderson, Mason, & Shirey, 1984). The solution is to establish a systematic process for giving an equal distribution of turns to read orally. The value of oral reading also depends in part on how the teacher deals with mistakes. A sensible rule of thumb is to ignore mistakes unless they disrupt the meaning of the text. If a teacher is compulsive about always correcting the smallest errors, children may become frustrated. When a child makes an oral reading mistake that changes the meaning, an effective strategy is to first wait and see if the child can come up with the right word without assistance. If not, focus the student's attention to clues about the word or its meaning. When the word has been identified correctly (with or without help), encourage the child to reread the entire sentence. Teachers who routinely supply the correct word immediately or solicit responses from other students get children in the habit of waiting passively for help.

Word Bank

English is not a phonemically exact language. Because of the imperfections in the relationship between some letters and sounds in words, the word bank plays an important role. These imperfections are most apparent in the high-frequency words studied in the word bank. Reading speed increases as accuracy in recognizing high-frequency words increases (Samuels & Kamil, 1984).

The word bank, a store of known words, is an essential part of the lesson plan until the students in the group automatically recognize at least 100 sight words. Sight words are the words most often seen in print and do not necessarily follow phonetic rules. Researchers (Bodrova, Leong, & Semenov, 1998) have documented the 100 most frequent sight words in books for beginning readers, which are included in the word bank (see Appendix D, p. 240). Unlike most word banks, this word bank consists of words that most students in the group recognize automatically. After 20 words are placed in the bank, 15 are sent home or to the word work center, and then the bank builds back up to 20 words. The words included in the bank are identified by students in books, word study, or sentence writing. After the word bank is completed in Stage 3, there is a transition in the focus of the word bank to include specialized vocabulary or tricky words. Teachers may choose to introduce these words before a selection is read or add them to the word bank as the students encounter them in the text. Along with word study, the word bank is an important tool used to establish automatic word recognition.

Word Study

The two largest tasks for students in the reading process are decoding and comprehension. In order for a student to begin the comprehension process, he or she must first learn to decode words. The purpose of word study is not to teach students to sound out words but to give students strategies so they learn to recognize words quickly and automatically, thereby increasing their reading fluency and comprehension.

Although the routine for the word study component will be reviewed in chapters 4 through 8, it is important to examine the significance of word study in the reading process. According to Adams (1990), the most critical factor behind fluent word reading is the ability to recognize letters, spelling patterns, and whole words effortlessly. Additionally, Chall (1967) states that the ability to use phonics seems to depend on whether or how a child has been taught phonics. Chall points out that when phonics are taught explicitly and systematically, not only kindergartners, but even preschoolers and special education students, can successfully use this method to learn new words. Other studies support this research, which indicates that explicit, systematic phonics instruction is the singularly successful mode of teaching young or slow learners (see Flesch, 1955).

The word study or word sorting activity included in each lesson teaches students how to recognize patterns in words, not just how to sound out words. Conversely, many traditional phonics programs encourage students to see words in parts, which hinders the learning process by asking students to sound out each letter.

Traditional reading instruction often ignores the significant relationship between word study and a student's reading level. Should a student be expected to master the silent *e* long-vowel pattern in spelling when he or she is at a beginning reading level? A child should never be expected to spell a word that he or she cannot read. In the Small-Group Differentiated Reading Model, spelling is included as a part of word study and is developed incrementally with a child's reading level. A sequence for reading stages and associated word study appears in Appendix D (p. 245).

Word study begins with students becoming confident in alphabet recognition while concurrently developing phonological awareness in hearing beginning sounds. In a review of research, Stanovich (1986) concluded that phonemic awareness is a more potent predictor of reading achievement than nonverbal intelligence, vocabulary, or listening comprehension. Much of the word study sequence in the Small-Group Differentiated Reading Model is adapted from Morris's (1999) *The Howard Street Tutoring Manual*. Each word study lesson begins with a sorting activity. This is followed by a matching game called Concentration, a spell check, or a word scramble. The lessons then move sequentially through beginning and ending consonant sounds, followed by short-vowel word families (common rimes). Phonics rules are very inconsistent, but sounds are stable in the part of the word from the vowel forward. Long-vowel patterns and variant-vowel patterns conclude the word study, which is useful for students reading at late first- and second-grade levels. The word study sequence is shown in Figure 9. A word study log for tracking student progress in word study is included in Appendix D (see p. 243).

The goal in word study is to provide young readers with the knowledge to give them effortless recognition of words. Word study is not an instructional program but an instructional process. This differentiated word study model provides teachers with a routine for presenting lessons to students in an effective compare-and-contrast strategy. Although there are no phonics rules to be memorized, children are encouraged to discover spelling patterns in the language. The word sort approach used in this model allows children to develop accuracy and fluency without the use of workbooks or

FIGURE 9
Word Study Sequence

1. Alphabet Recognition (upper- and lowercase)

2. Consonants (beginning and ending)

3. Short-Vowel Word Families

1	2	3	4	5
a	i	o	u	e
-at	-it	-ot	-ut	-et
-an	-ig	-op	-ug	-ed
-ap	-in	-ob	-un	-en
-ack	-ick	-ock	-uck	-ell

4. Short Vowels

a	i	o	u	e
bad	pig	mom	bus	pet

5. Vowel Patterns—Level 1

a	i	o	u	e
cat	hid	mom	mud	red
make	ride	rope	cute	feet
car	girl	for	hurt	her
day		go	blue	he
		boat		
		look		
		cow		

6. Vowel Patterns—Level 2

a	i	o	u	e
rain	right	told		meat
ball	by	moon		head
saw	find	boil		new
		low		
		loud		
		boy		

ditto sheets. Word study includes game-like sorting activities that are short, challenging, and engaging for children. Word sort instructions and sequence are included in Appendix D (p. 242).

Writing

The Learning First Alliance (1998), an organization of 12 U.S. national education associations, states that writing, in addition to being valuable in its own right, gives children the opportunities to use their new reading competence. When taught appropriately, the processes of reading and writing go hand in hand (Butler & Clay, 1982). In the Small-Group Differentiated Reading Model, sentences geared to a group's word study level provide the material for a writing experience. Written texts demonstrate standard form and spelling for young writers (Bean & Bouffler, 1997). For example, if the reading group is working on the *A* family in word study, the target sentence would include some words from the *A* family along with some high-frequency words from the word bank. With assistance from students, the teacher writes the sentence and demonstrates concepts of print such as capital letters, spacing, and punctuation. After the sentence is completed, the teacher writes the sentence on a sentence strip, cuts the words in the sentence apart, and asks the students to assist in reconstructing the sentence. This allows students to use strategies such as looking at beginning sounds in words, noticing capital letters, and recognizing high-frequency words. After the students have developed the skills necessary to write a sentence independently, the sentence-strip sequence is dropped. At this point, a sentence is dictated by the teacher, and the students write it independently. Linking reading and writing encourages students to practice known strategies that build confidence.

New Read

The more time spent reading books at an appropriate instructional level, the more students achieve (Rosenshine, 1978). There is a real need for students to be engaged in "real" reading while applying their knowledge in reading situations. Real reading can be said to take place when the parts are put together in a smooth, orchestrated performance. The most useful form of practice is reading meaningful text for the purpose of understanding the messages it contains.

To acquire reading fluency, students must have enough guided practice for reading to become automatic. Practice is the key to building automaticity. There is strong evidence to support that students who spend a lot of time reading become good readers (Allington, 1977; Stanovich, 1986). The new read allows students to explore a new text daily in a supported environment where feedback encourages growth.

Each reading lesson ends with the introduction and reading of a new book. Before reading, students are encouraged to predict the story line by looking at the book's illustrations. Then, with the teacher's assistance, the students modify their original predictions while they read the story. The routine of introducing a new book each day provides students with the opportunity to read five new books every week. The new book should be slightly more difficult than previous reads. Using carefully leveled books allows children to progress at their instructional level—challenged but not overwhelmed. Appropriately pacing children through increasingly difficult reading material is one key to effective instruction. However, the process of purchasing or organizing a leveled book collection to support the reading model can be a formidable task.

Selecting Leveled Books for Small-Group Differentiated Reading Instruction

During the past several years, the need to level books for beginning readers has become more apparent to educators. Leveled books serve as the centerpiece for the Small-Group Differentiated Reading Model, and publishing companies have become increasingly aware of their importance. There are a variety of models for leveling books including Reading Recovery, Developmental Reading Assessment, Fountas and Pinnell, and others by individual textbook companies. Selecting quality, accurately leveled books is critical to the differentiated reading process. Each individual school should decide on a leveling system that is expansive and appropriate for the books available. At that point, all books should be merged using the same leveling system. Books should be previewed to make sure that the levels seem appropriate for beginning readers. There should be some balance between more natural language books and controlled vocabulary books. Natural language books use language familiar to children to tell a complete story. Controlled vocabulary books use sets of words chosen according to the frequency they appear in language and books and words that demonstrate sound relationships in phonics instruction. These controlled vocabulary stories must rely heavily on picture support for meaning.

Selecting beginning books for children is a balancing act between natural language and controlled vocabulary books. Children have an easier time understanding stories written in familiar (natural) language but may have difficulty decoding some of the challenging words. Using controlled vocabulary in stories can be boring and unengaging for students. The answer for the most effective reading instruction is to provide a balance between these two book types.

Therefore, choosing books from a variety of sources is encouraged, as long as books are eventually leveled using the same system. A book need not be permanently slotted as a level 7 or level 8. After using the book with children, teacher teams should review books that might seem inappropriately leveled. Leveling books is a somewhat subjective activity, and there are no clearly wrong or right decisions in assigning levels.

The following criteria provide a basic framework for examining and leveling books:

- overall length of the book
- number of words on a page
- number of lines on a page
- correspondence of illustrations to print
- legibility of type
- size of print
- spacing between words and between lines
- phonic complexity
- range of punctuation
- range of illustrations
- familiarity of content
- familiarity of theme
- complexity of story line
- type of text: narrative or expository
- repetitive language
- sentence structure
- vocabulary

Table 2 is presented as a guide for selecting leveled books to support the five stages of the Small-Group Differentiated Reading Model. A range of appropriate book levels is suggested. Many textbook companies level books using the three most popular systems—Reading Recovery, Fountas and Pinnell, and Developmental Reading Assessment, which are reflected in Table 2. In the past, teachers have labored over leveling book collections, but as this process becomes easier, it is critical that teachers be familiar with their leveled books so that they are aware of the unique supports and challenges included in each text.

Effectively Engaging the Other Students During Small-Group Reading Instruction

Perhaps the most frequently asked question by teachers eager to implement small-group reading in their classrooms is, What is the rest of the class doing? To adequately address the question, it is important to recall the previous discussion in chapter 1 concerning balanced literacy. More explicitly, which parts of balanced literacy could best be implemented during this time segment? This time is best spent on reading and writing activities that students need to practice on their own. What better time to do this than during reading groups? Developing and managing these activities then becomes the focus. Throughout this book, suggestions for literacy centers (Literacy Center Alerts)

TABLE 2
Leveled Books for Reading Groups

Stage	Reading Recovery	DRA	Fountas & Pinnell
1 Emergent Reader	1–2	A–2	A–B
2 Beginning Reader	3–5	3–5	C–D
3 Fledgling Reader	6–11	6–10	E–G
4 Transitional Reader	12–16	11–17	H–I
5 Independent Reader	17–20 +	18–28	J–M

will be given to support the various stages of reading. Independent activities must be at the appropriate developmental level. Activities that are too difficult will cause frustration and possible discipline problems. Additionally, the activities should be teacher friendly and not too labor intensive to construct or grade.

Developing a Routine

From the first day of school, begin acclimating your students to working independently. Start with short time periods and perhaps do only one or two parts of the small-group reading lesson. Make sure that everyone understands rule number one: Never disturb the teacher during reading group unless someone is sick or injured. Try placing a strip of tape on the rug close to your group and tell students to stand on the tape if there is an emergency. If you see that the students are not sick or injured, let them stand there. After a while, they will return to their activities. Other suggestions to prevent interruptions include the following:

- Keep a small lamp on your table. If the light is on, students should not disturb the teacher.
- Put on a funny hat when you are in reading group. This will act as a signal that you are not to be disturbed.
- Be clear about instructions and expectations. Student must know what to do if they finish an activity early.

Organization

Organizing and managing the class for small-group reading requires some thought. The classroom usually operates best when there is a mixture of assigned tasks, literacy center activities, and follow-up assignments from the small-group reading instruction.

Teacher-Assigned Tasks

There are clearly a number of options for assigning tasks. The first group of activities is referred to as teacher tasks. This simply means that students are expected to be in their seats to complete these tasks required by the teacher. Generally, these tasks need to be achievable for all students in your class. The following are some examples:

- Write five sentences for five spelling words.
- Respond to a shared reading completed earlier in the day through writing, art, or drama.
- Complete a short math activity.
- Practice handwriting (a great time for students to complete this is after a demonstration using the overhead).
- Write and illustrate a story.
- Complete journal writing activities.

As students finish their assignments there should be an established place to put the completed assignments. Then, students should be allowed to move to the next activity. Never require students to sit needlessly or wait for a rotation bell to ring. This will lead to boredom and potential discipline problems.

Managing Literacy Centers

Another group of activities takes place in literacy centers. Establish a routine for managing literacy centers by assigning some tasks for the day or week and allowing some free choices. The following literacy centers should constantly be available for students in K–2 classrooms.

- **Book center**—A variety of books should be available and categorized according to reading level or subject area. The group "rereads" for the week can be stored in this location for independent reading. Have students keep a log of the books they read in the book center. The Reading Log (see Appendix D, p. 241) is one way to assess the books read.
- **Word work center**—This center should contain activities that are leveled and support the small-group word study. A "tub" of activities should be available for each reading group containing word study cards, word bank cards, and cut-up sentences to be put back together.
- **Spelling center**—This center is easy to create, and children of all ages and abilities enjoy its variety. Post the weekly spelling words or word study words. Have children visit the center to work on spelling words in a variety of ways including
    - tracing words in sand,
    - making words with clay,
    - using sticks to make words,
    - using dry erase boards, or
    - tracing words in shaving cream.
- **Recording center**—Set up a tape recorder for children to practice reading into and then have them listen to what they have recorded. This develops fluency and encourages self-assessment. Students can read the word wall, spelling words, or a short story to practice their reading skills.
- **Listening center**—Listening to a recorded book is one of the best activities available to support literacy development (see Figure 10). This activity promotes the development of critical comprehension skills in beginning readers. The Listening Center Log (see Appendix D, p. 242) makes the students accountable for completing the activity. Figure 11 shows a completed Listening Center Log.

FIGURE 10
A Student Listens to a Recorded Book in the Listening Center

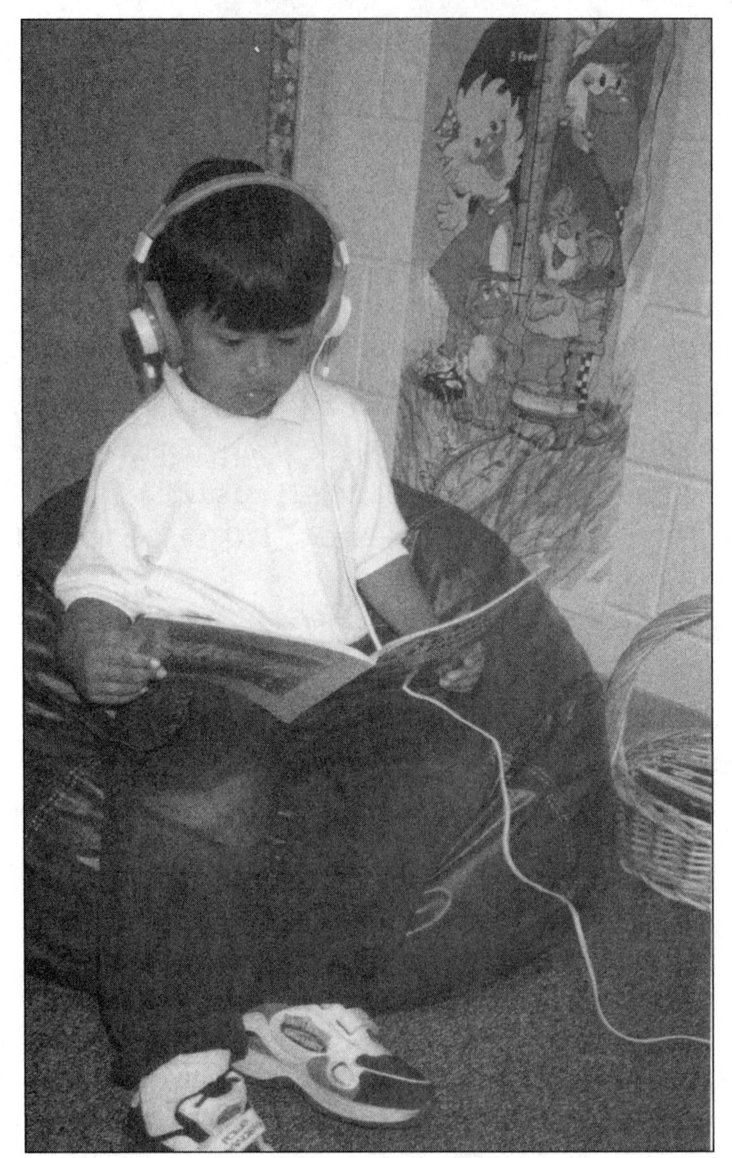

- **Computer center**—Independent time spent on the computer is a great way to engage students appropriately. Make sure that the activities on the computer support the student's individual achievement level. Computer programs that support word study, writing, or reading appropriate leveled books are some examples.
- **Art center**—Don't overlook this important area. Allow students to use art as a way to respond to reading and writing activities. Students enjoy decorating poems, pieces of shared writing, independent writing, and cards or making something special for a friend.

FIGURE 11
Completed Listening Center Log

Date 2-26-03.

I listened to LadyBug

This is a picture of my favorite part.

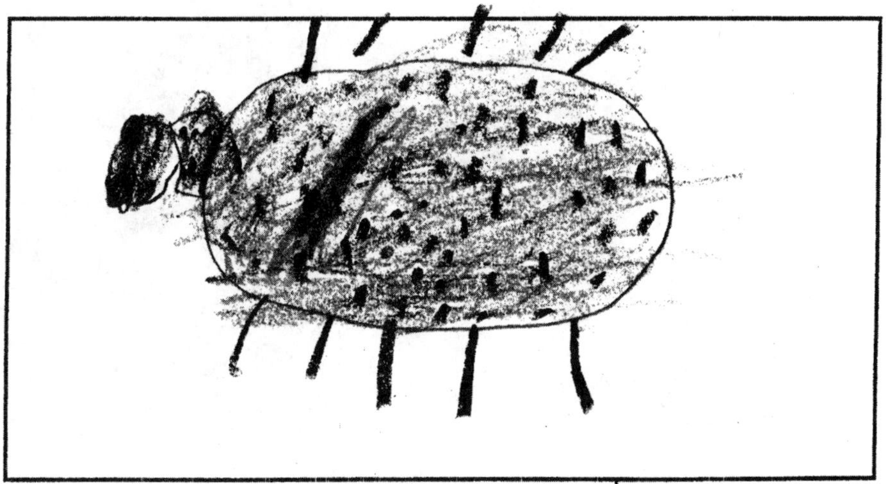

My favorite part was some bugs are red with spots on their back.

- **Read the Room**—All you need here is a funny pair of glasses and a pointer (see Figure 12). Students are given the opportunity to roam the room reading stories, poems, and word walls. It is the teacher's responsibility to maintain a print-rich environment, and, best of all, there is nothing for the teacher to grade.
- **Write the Room**—Place a variety of pencils, paper, and clipboards in a basket. Students explore the room and copy print that they want to write down or take home. Poems, songs, and stories are especially popular pieces that students like to copy.
- **Writing center**—This is the place where assigned or independent writing can take place. Lists of words are a must, along with an alphabet chart. The word wall

FIGURE 12
A Student "Reads the Room"

should be in close proximity to encourage students to write stories, notes, or letters. Have a variety of paper types and colors available along with numerous writing utensils to make this center a hit.

Work in literacy centers can be assigned by the teacher or presented as free choices to students. During a five-day week, a mixture of five assigned centers and five "free" centers could be included. This will allow the teacher to quickly organize a schedule of activities that will actively involve students while they work independently on their literacy skills. An alternative would be to assign two centers each day. Please note that students not meeting for reading group on a particular day may have more time to complete assignments. Never penalize students involved in reading group by asking them to do all the work assigned to the rest of the class. Be fair in your expectations for all your students.

Figure 13 shows two ways of assigning literacy centers for the day. The circle chart allows each group (color coded) to attend two literacy centers daily. The square chart simply uses popsicle sticks to assign students to literacy centers.

FIGURE 13
Two Ways to Assign Literacy Centers

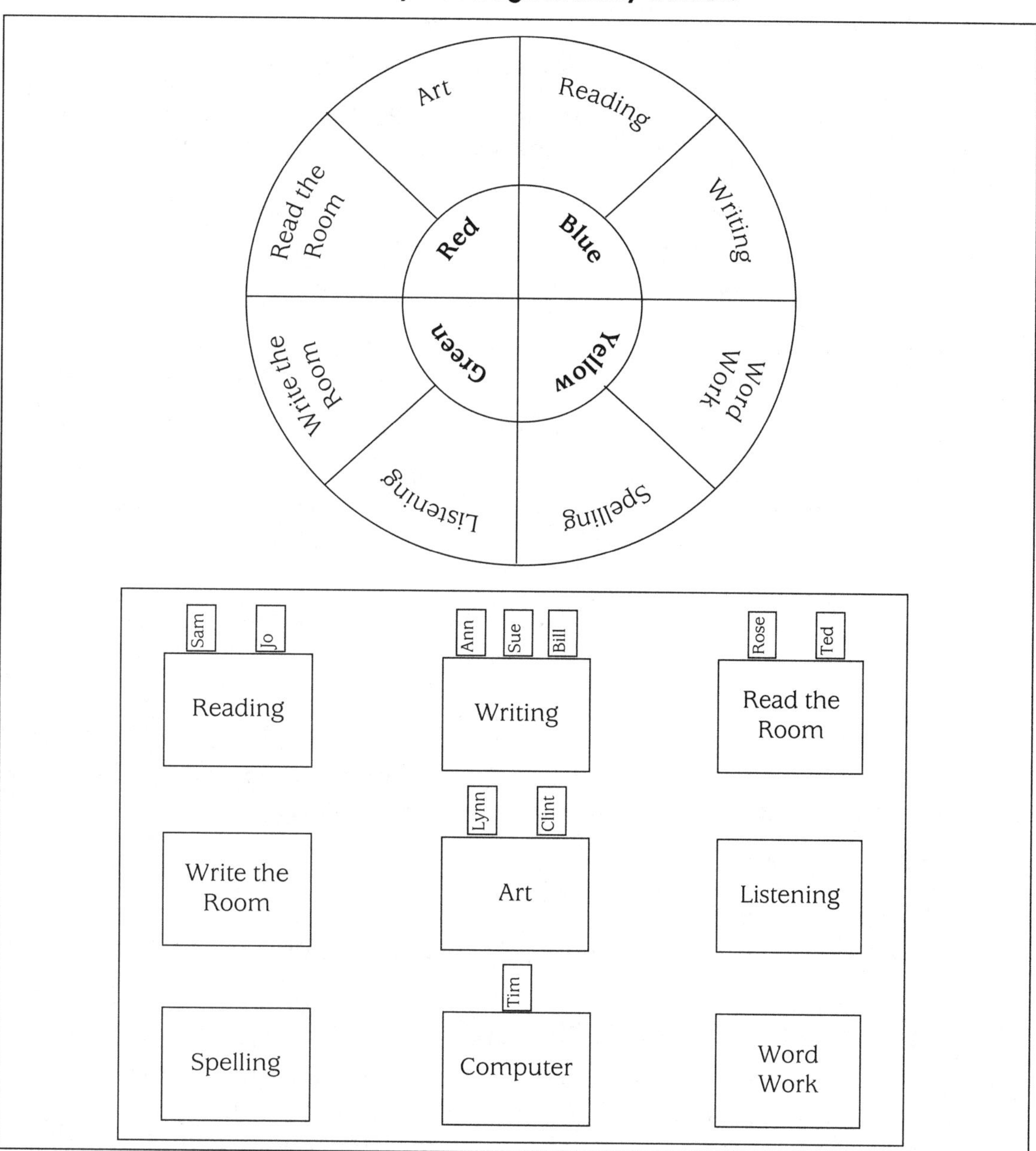

Follow-Up to Small-Group Reading

A third group of activities can be devised as a follow-up to each small-group reading lesson. As you finish with a reading group, the students should routinely complete a follow-up assignment based on their reading level. One assignment could be to reread the new book with a partner or individually. There can be no better use of time than to reread. Additionally, in the early stages of reading, students could illustrate the journal sentence or glue the sentence in order as a part of their follow-up to the reading

FIGURE 14
Reading Group Follow-Up (Independent Work)

Monday	Tuesday	Wednesday	Thursday	Friday
Cut word sort (individual run on ditto paper to keep in envelopes)	Partner sort (use individual word study cards)	Play Concentration with a partner (use word study cards)	Play Concentration with a partner	Sort and paste word study (use as an assessment)
Paste the cut-up sentence in the journal. Illustrate the sentence.	Paste the cut-up sentence in the journal. Illustrate the sentence.	Paste the cut-up sentence in the journal. Illustrate the sentence.	Paste the cut-up sentence in the journal. Illustrate the sentence.	Paste the cut-up sentence in the journal. Illustrate the sentence.
Reread the new book.	Read the new book with a partner.	Write in reading response journal. Write a sentence. Draw a picture.	Read the new book with a partner.	Free read

group. Teachers do not need to feel guilty if there are no papers to grade as a result of students' independent work. Figure 14 is a model for a kindergarten class for follow-up to the reading group. Other suggestions for follow-up include

- looking for word bank words in books,
- writing sentences with words in word study, and
- responding to the new read through writing, drama, or art work.

Managing the Challenging Student

Every class includes one or two students who lack the self-discipline to move independently. These students work best in a quiet spot in close proximity to the teacher. Teacher-assigned tasks should be used and centers should not be an option unless the literacy center activities can be brought to the student's area. This also allows for "timeout" for disruptive students or students not completing assignments by isolating them from the rest of the group. Students generally enjoy independence and respond negatively when their freedom is taken away.

Conclusion

The components outlined in the Small-Group Differentiated Reading Model provide focused instruction in basic literacy elements. Unlike traditional guided reading models, writing and word study are included as important parts of the daily lesson plan. Additionally, the reading and rereading of appropriately leveled texts provides the centerpiece for small-group reading instruction. The components in the Small-Group Differentiated Reading Model work congruently to provide a solid foundation for continued literacy growth.

Perhaps the biggest obstacle facing teachers in the implementation of this model is the task of keeping students purposefully engaged as they work independently during small-group reading time. Although teachers could have students work solely on completing worksheets or board work, a plan that also includes teacher tasks, literacy centers, and follow-up assignments from the small-group reading might prove to be more beneficial. These activities provide a time for focused, independent practice in reading and writing that is essential in a balanced literacy program.

Teacher tasks are assignments that can be completed independently by the entire class and should be easily prepared and managed. Literacy centers, when structured appropriately, are open invitations to independent learning. As teachers develop these literacy center activities, they should consider activities that are differentiated to meet a wide range of learners. Additionally, activities that require minimum preparation and supervision also should be considered. Assignments that follow the small groups allow for practice specific to the needs of the individual groups. Selecting an appropriate management system during this time also is critical to successful implementation. With careful planning and the development of classroom routines, this structure gives teachers large blocks of uninterrupted instructional time with small groups of students.

CHAPTER 4

Stage 1: Emergent Reader

Characteristics of Emergent Readers

According to the *Oxford Illustrated American Dictionary*, *emergent* means "becoming apparent, to come into view when formerly concealed" (1998, p. 226). Emergent readers are beginning to exhibit some characteristics of early readers. They are typically beginning to midyear kindergartners who recognize less than half the alphabet. In some cases, they may know none of the alphabet letters. As stated previously, it is important to determine the letters each student knows for grouping purposes. Another characteristic of emergent readers is their inability to track print or point to each word as they read. Finally, emergent readers generally lack phonemic awareness; they are unable to attend to individual sounds within spoken words. Emergent readers have special needs in the area of written language learning that are difficult to meet in the context of whole-class instruction.

Texts for Emergent Readers

It is important to expose emergent readers to text right away to support their reading efforts and to affirm them in the belief that they will become readers. Enlarged text is helpful for emergent readers. This text can be in the form of a Big Book, poem, song, or student-generated story. The structure must be simple so that pictures tell the story. For emergent readers, one or two sentences per page are appropriate. It is important that the text be repetitive, with only one or two word changes on each page. Rhyming within the text also is helpful in supporting emergent readers. Nursery rhymes and familiar chants are excellent resources for these students because the familiarity makes the task of tracking print easier. Also, nursery rhymes (for example, "Peas Porridge") often contain a number of high-frequency words (e.g., *hot*, *cold*, *in*, *the*, *days*, *old*):

Peas Porridge
Peas porridge hot,
Peas porridge cold,
Peas porridge in the pot,
Nine days old.

Student-generated stories, in which each group member contributes a sentence, also may serve as appropriate texts. Students can dictate an original story, or the teacher can provide a structure and let the children fill in the blanks.

I like to play tag.
I like to play ball.
I like to play soccer.
I like to play tennis.
I like to play games.
I like to play ______.

Whatever the text, it will be the new read used for emergent readers the first day and the reread for days two and three. Rotating Big Books, poems, songs, and student-generated stories provides variety and keeps the students' attention. In consideration of those who choose to use individual leveled texts, the following are book levels appropriate for emergent readers:

Leveling System	**Book Levels**
Reading Recovery	1–2
DRA	A–2
Fountas and Pinnell	A–B

When most students are able to track simple sentences, these individual books will take the place of enlarged text.

Instructional Strategies in the Emergent Reader Lesson Plan

Rereading

Begin by rereading yesterday's new read. Initially, the teacher provides full support during the rereading by using a strategy called echo reading. The teacher reads the first page, then the students read the same page together as the teacher points to each word on an enlarged text; if individual books are used, students point to text. The second page of the story is read in the same way. After several pages of echo reading, the students are encouraged to read independently, with the teacher providing as little support as necessary. Echo supported reading on the first several pages is important to get students "into the story," providing them with character names and repetitive sentence patterns used in the book. Although this is a reread from the day before, this technique is still useful for a successful reread of the story. Usually, the hardest part of the story for emergent readers is the first few pages. Therefore, providing this up-front support makes good sense.

- Read a page, and then have different student groups echo read together. (For example, ask girls to read a page and boys to read the next page.) When a group of students reads a passage together, it is referred to as choral reading.
- Finger point to each word as students read or have students finger point in their individual books.
- After completing a page, point to a word and let students track up to the word in order to identify it. Suppose the sentence is *The fish is in the lake*. After reading the sentence together (chorally), point to the word *in*. Then, ask, "What's this

FIGURE 15
Reading Lesson Plan: Emergent Reader (Stage 1)

Group:______________________________ Date:______________

Rereading Level	Comments
1.______________________ 2.______________________	
Word Bank	
Word Study Alphabet Focus (Matching)____________ Concentration______________ or Spell Check______________	
Writing (Cut-Up Sentence) ______________________	
New Read Level 1.______________________	

Small-Group Reading Instruction: A Differentiated Teaching Model for Beginning and Struggling Readers by Beverly Tyner © 2004. Newark, DE: International Reading Association. May be copied for classroom use.

word?" If there is no response, ask the students to read the sentence again, but this time to whisper read it in a quiet voice until they get to the unknown word. When the students reach the unknown word in their reading, they say it in a louder voice. This is referred to as "tracking up to a word" and encourages the development of concept of word.

- If you point to a word that most students recognize without tracking up to the word, add it to the word bank, because the students recognize it automatically.

As the students gain familiarity with the texts, reduce support during the rereading.

- Have students choral read without your support (or with as little support as necessary).
- Ask individual students to finger point to the enlarged text (Big Book, rhyme, or story) for the group as they read. (Assist students if necessary or have students read from their individual copies of leveled books.)
- Invite individual students to read pages.
- Rotate reading by individuals with choral reading.

Teacher: Yesterday, we read the nursery rhyme *Mary Had a Little Lamb*. Let's try reading that again today. I'll point to the words, and we can read together. Do you remember how it starts?

(The teacher points as the students read together.)

Mary had a little lamb,
Its fleece was white as snow.
And everywhere that Mary went,
The lamb was sure to go.

Teacher: That was great. Sarah, will you point this time while we read the poem together?

(Rhyme is read again.)

Teacher: (Going back to the word *had*) Do you know this word?

(Four of the six students correctly identify the word.)

Teacher: I think that this is a word for our word bank. Let me write it on a card while you spell it for me.

Teacher: Now let's read the book we've been working on for a few days. This will be the last day that we read *Big Sea Animals* (Smith, Giles, & Randell, 2000a). Let's see how many of the sea animals we can remember in this book before we start.

Nick: There are sharks and whales and dolphins.

Teacher: Good. Do you remember any others?

FIGURE 16
Students Illustrate Stories in the Art Center

Beth: Yes. There is an octopus.

(The teacher distributes individual books.)

Teacher: Now let's read the book. I think that you can read most of it by yourself if you look at the pictures to help you. I'll get you started. (Teacher reads first page while students follow along and then asks students to echo read. Students complete the book as the teacher calls on groups or individuals to read a page.)

LITERACY CENTER ALERT

Take the poems, songs, and student stories to the art center (for definitions of literacy centers, see chapter 3, pp. 43–46), and let students illustrate them (see Figure 16). Be sure to keep copies in the book center. Try tape recording the texts and letting the students finger-point read along with the tape.

Word Bank

Using the 100 Most Frequent Words in Books for Beginning Readers as a guide (see Appendix D, p. 240), begin a word bank for the group.

- Look for words in stories or sentences that most students recognize, and write them on index cards. Make a big deal out of it; for example, say, "Wow! I think this is a word we can put in our word bank."

- Flash the word bank words to the group for automatic recognition, or call on individual students. Remember, these should be words that most of the students in the group can recognize automatically.
- Slowly build the word bank. Emergent readers may need more time between words than more advanced readers. The number of words added each week will depend on the children's readiness to hold sight words in memory.
- Use the chart Watch Our Sight Words Grow (see Appendix D, p. 239) to track word bank progress.

Teacher: Now that we have added the new word *had* to our word bank, let's count the words and see how many we have.

(Teacher and students count together; emergent readers should recognize at least 10 sight words in this emergent reader stage.)

Teacher: Wow! Now we have six words that we know. I'm going to show you these words one at a time. As soon as you recognize the word, tell me what it is.

(Teacher observes group responses. If a particular word is a struggle for most of the group, the teacher should remove the word and try to add it back at a later time.)

STOP

LITERACY CENTER ALERT

- Put word bank words in a sealable plastic bag, and leave them in the word work center for students to practice reading with a partner.
- Post a list of the word bank words in the writing center. Color-code each group's words.
- Include word bank words on the word wall.

Word Study

Alphabet Focus (Matching)

Begin word study for emergent readers by reviewing the ERSI and determining which alphabet letters most students in the group know.

- Select two letters that students know and three letters that they do not know.
- Using the upper- and lowercase letter cards provided (see Appendix B, pp. 133–134), have students match lowercase letters to uppercase letters. Be sure to have the children say the letter names as many times as possible. Always use two known letters to give students confidence. If you find that five letters are too challenging, reduce the number of letters to four.

Teacher:	Let's take a look at some alphabet letters that we have been working on. (Teacher places the first letter *S* on the table.) Who remembers the name of this letter?
Patrick:	That's an *S*.
Teacher:	Good job. (Teacher continues until there are five uppercase letters [*B*, *M*, *S*, *F*, and *A*] on the table—two that most of the group know and three that most of the group do not readily recognize.)

Teacher:	These are all uppercase, or capital, letters. Now let's see if we can match them with the lowercase letters. Sarah, where would this letter go?

(Sarah correctly places the lowercase *s* under the uppercase *S*.)

Teacher:	Good. What is the name of this letter?
Sarah:	*S*.
Teacher:	Yes. We have an uppercase *S* and a lowercase *s*.

(This process continues as the teacher asks students to match the remaining letters.)

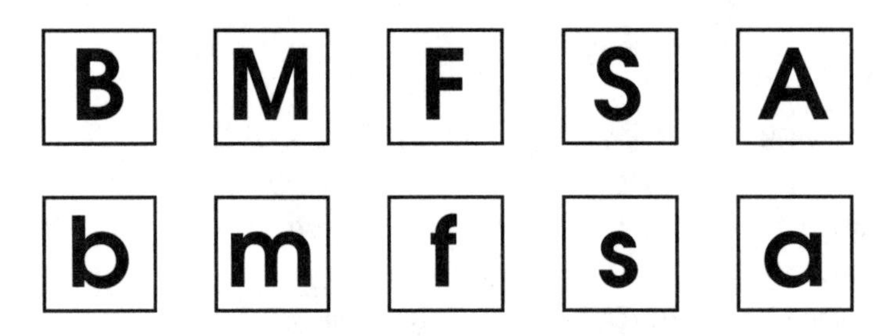

This activity reviews the letter names that need to be committed to memory and should be done daily. The next two activities should be alternated every other day because there will not be enough time to do both.

Concentration

After matching the upper- and lowercase letters, quickly turn over the 10 cards and mix them up. Ask each student to turn over one card, say the name of the letter on the card, and try to find a match by turning over another card. If a student gets a match and can name the letter, he or she gets an extra turn. If there is no match, the next player gets a turn. This game can be played on a tray and moved from player to player (see Figure 17). Small magnets and a magnetic board also can be used. Another option is to use three sets of playing cards and monitor three pairs of students playing. This will allow students to have more opportunities to actively participate.

FIGURE 17
Students Play Concentration

Teacher: Now I'm going to turn over these letters and mix them up so we can play a game of Concentration. Ben, you can take the first turn. Remember to watch Ben so you will know where the letters are when it's your turn.

(Ben turns over the letter *F*.)

Teacher: What letter did you get?

Ben: *F*.

Teacher: Yes. It is a capital *F*. Now turn over another card to see if you can find the lowercase *f*.

(Ben turns over the letter card *B*.)

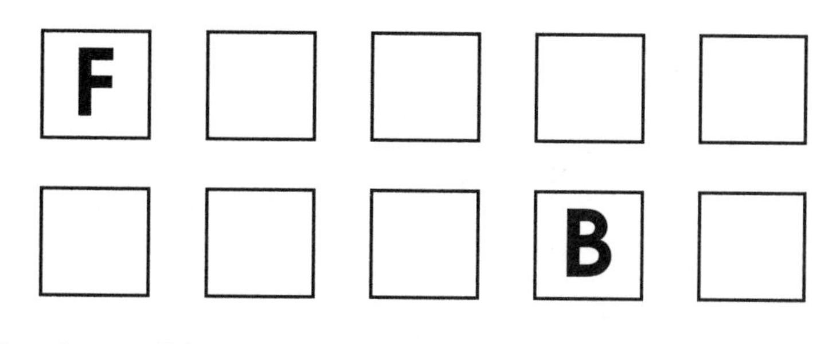

Teacher: What letter did you get?

Ben: *B*.

Teacher: Is that a match?

Ben: No.

Teacher: No, it isn't a match, so we will turn both letters back over. Remember where those two letters are.

(This process continues until all matches are made.)

Spell Check

Spell Check for emergent readers is simply the production of the alphabet letters being studied (see Figure 18). Spell Check can be done in an individual student journal constructed with newsprint on the inside and construction paper for the cover. Individual dry erase boards also can be used for Spell Check.

- Randomly call out the five letters being studied, and have students write the letters one at a time in their journals or on the dry erase boards. If necessary, leave the letter cards out so students can have as much support as needed. Gradually take the cards away as students become more confident in writing the letters independently.
- Don't be concerned with correct letter formation or if students write an upper- or lowercase letter. You will not have time to go through all the lesson plan components if you spend too much time on these areas now.

Teacher: Let's practice writing some of these alphabet letters. (Teacher distributes dry erase boards and markers or pencils and paper. The five uppercase letters are left on the table because this group is still struggling with letter formation and identification.)

Teacher: Is everybody ready? The first letter that I want you to write is *S*. It can be an upper- or a lowercase *S*. If you aren't sure what an *S* looks like, look at the letters on the table and find the letter.

FIGURE 18
Spell Check Example

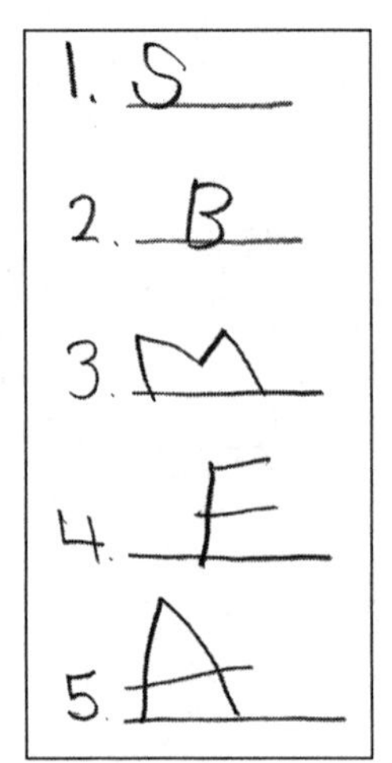

(Several students immediately write the letter *S*, while other students search the cards.)

Teacher: Susan, do you need a little help getting started? (Teacher reaches over and makes an *S* for Susan. Then, she asks Susan to make another *S*.)

Teacher: Good. If you wrote the letter *S* (teacher holds up the letter card), give yourself a check (✓). (The teacher does not check the letter with the group until everyone has successfully written an *S* so all students experience success, even if teacher assistance is needed.)

(Exercise continues as the students write the five target letters. As students become more confident in recognizing and writing these letters, the letter cards are removed during Spell Check.)

STOP

LITERACY CENTER ALERT

- Put the letter cards in the word work center for students or partners to play Concentration.
- Put dry erase boards and markers in the writing center to practice writing the letters being studied.
- Only include letters that have been introduced to the group.
- Use letter tiles, magnetic letters, sandpaper letters, and so forth to reinforce the letters being studied.

Writing

- Post a sentence strip so that it is easily visible to the group. (If you can write upside down, you can put the sentence strip on the table in front of the students.)
- Choose a simple four- or five-word sentence that relates to something pertinent to the group (see the following examples).

We	went	to	the	park	.

We	like	to	play	games	.

We	are	learning	about	frogs	.

We	have	a	pet	fish	.

Obey	the	rules	at	school	.

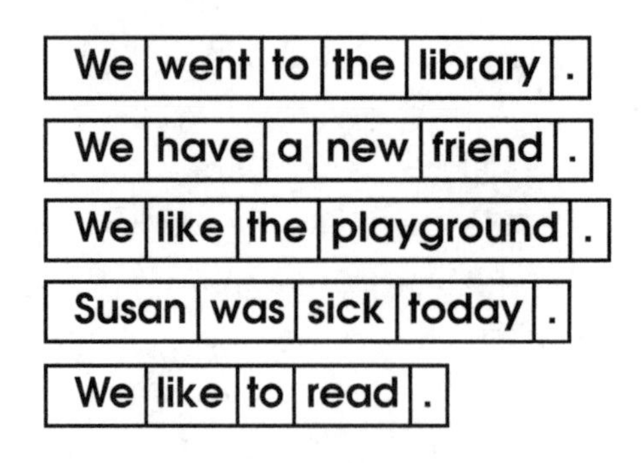

- Repeat the sentence for the group at least three times before you start writing. Have the students repeat the sentence with you. Point to your fingers in a left-to-right progression, and count the number of words in the sentence. The students should repeat the sentence several times until it is committed to memory.
- Ask the students, "What is the first word in the sentence?" Write the word on the strip.
- As you continue writing the words, emphasize such things as starting with a capital letter, finger spacing between words, and punctuation at the end of the sentence. Because these students are working on alphabet recognition, ask the students to identify letters as you write them. Talk aloud as you write. For example, you could state, "This is the first letter of the first word in the sentence, so I capitalize it."
- After completing the sentence, cut the words apart and give individual students a word or punctuation mark from the sentence. Make sure that each student has a part of the sentence. If there aren't enough pieces for all students in the group, the remaining student(s) can actually put the sentence back together.
- Then, ask, "Who has the first word in the sentence?" Continue until the sentence is complete.

Choose words that contain letters that previously have been introduced to the group. Repeat high-frequency words that could become word bank words, and use no more than five words in a sentence. For reinforcement, choose words that have letters currently being learned in word study.

Teacher: We have all been excited about the snow this week, so I thought that we would write a sentence about it. Listen to our sentence for today: *We had a big snow.* (This sentence is selected because it contains two words from the group's word bank along with words that contain some letters the group is focusing on in word study.)

Teacher: Listen again: *We had a big snow.* (Teacher repeats the sentence and points to her fingers in a left-to-right progression while the students observe.)

Teacher: How many words are in our sentence? Let's count them together. (Teacher and students count words together.)

Teacher: Now hold up your left hand and say the sentence with me while you touch your fingers.

Teacher: Now let's write this sentence together. (Teacher places a sentence strip on the table or board, and the sentence is written so that the students can see it.)

Teacher: What is the first word in the sentence?

Jennifer: *We*.

Teacher: Yes, *We* is the first word. What kind of letter do we always start a sentence with?

Harrison: A capital letter.

Teacher: That's right. So I'm going to make a capital *W*. Does anyone know how to spell the rest of the word *We*? Remember, *We* is one of our word bank words.

Leslie: W-e.

(Students contribute responses as the teacher writes the sentence.)

Teacher: Now I'm going to cut the sentence apart. Say the words as I cut them off. What is the first word?

Susan: *We*.

Teacher: Good. Susan remembered the word *We*.

(Teacher finishes cutting sentence apart and distributes the words to the students.)

Teacher: Now who has the first word of the sentence?

Robert: I do.

Teacher: Good, Robert.

(Exercise continues as sentence is assembled.)

Teacher: Now I'm going to put our sentence pieces is a plastic bag and write the sentence on the outside of the bag. It will be in your word study basket so that you can practice putting the sentence back together.

LITERACY CENTER ALERT

After finishing the cut-up sentence, place the sentence in a sealable plastic bag and write the sentence on the outside of the bag with a marker. Provide a pocket chart (or use the floor if necessary), and let students put the sentences together as an independent activity.

New Read

- Introduce a new book by doing a picture walk. Providing a picture walk is one way to support reading a new text. The picture walk also familiarizes the students with the story. It includes talking with students about each page of a book and discussing what the pictures tell about the story. (I do not include the last picture so students have a chance to predict what will happen.)
- Make text connections for students. (Have you ever read a book like this before? What do you already know?)
- Ask students to make predictions based on the picture walk. (What do you think is happening in this picture? [Turn the page.] Now what is happening?)
- Name the story characters as you do the picture walk.
- Point to a few words that might be difficult for the students to recognize.
- Read the book (or poem, song, etc.) to the group as you finger point to each word or have students follow along in individual groups. This kind of support reduces student anxiety and establishes a meaningful way to read the new text.
- Reread the book by allowing students to echo read the pages. As students read the text, they begin to mentally fill in the story line confirming and modifying predictions.

Many teachers get frustrated with emergent readers because they believe the students are simply memorizing the words, but the process of memorizing short sentences and pointing to words in a left-to-right progression is the first stage in the reading process.

Teacher: The last thing we will do today is take a look at our new book. (Teacher holds up cover of Big Book.) The name of our new book is *Playing Outside* (Smith, Giles, & Randell, 2000b). What do you like to play outside? (Teacher makes text connections)

Teacher: What kinds of things do you think the children in this book will play outside?

(Students make predictions.)

Teacher: Let's take a look at the pictures in this book. Look at the first page. What are the children doing on this page?

Gloria: Swinging.

Teacher: Yes, and this is the word *swinging*. (Teacher points to word.) What letter does the word *swinging* begin with?

Gloria: *S*.

Teacher: Yes, and *S* is a letter that we have been studying.

(Teacher remembers that the group is working on letter recognition and not ready for beginning consonant sounds.)

(Teacher continues the picture walk through the book pointing out picture clues and making text connections that will support the students in a successful read of the new book.)

Teacher: Now let's go back and read *Playing Outside*. I'll read the first page and you point to the words in your book while I read. When I finish reading, you will read the page to me. You will be my echo.

(After the first two or three pages are echo read and the repetitive story line is established, the students are encouraged to look at the picture clues and read the page with the teacher without echo reading.)

Teacher: (After the book is read) I'm going to go back and point to some words in the story to see if you know them. Do you know this word? (Teacher points to the word *and*.)

(Four of the six students automatically recognize the word.)

Teacher: I think we can put this word in our word bank tomorrow.

Teacher: Do you know this word? (Teacher points to the word *play*.)

(Students do not respond.)

Teacher: We can figure out this word if we whisper read up to this word. Let's try it. Do you remember how it started? We like to play. Yes, this word is *play*.

Teacher: We will read this book again tomorrow.

Comments

The lesson plan form includes space for teacher comments. Use this section to make notes on specific problems or successes. This will allow you to make decisions regarding the pace of instruction (i.e., whether to move forward or to review).

See Figure 19 for a completed lesson plan for emergent readers.

When to Move to the Next Stage

There is no precise way to decide when to move the reading group to Stage 2 because the Reading Review is not appropriate for emergent readers who are still learning to track print and are limited in word knowledge. Generally, most students in the group should be able to recognize and write at least half the alphabet letters. Additionally, the majority of the group also should be able to track simple lines of text. If some students' readiness is questionable, other options are available: Provide additional individual assistance with a tutor or older student, or allow the borderline students to meet with both a Stage 1 and a Stage 2 group for a time period to determine if they can move ahead successfully. It is better to move on to the next stage too quickly than to remain at a level at which students are left unchallenged. If the new stage presents too much of a challenge, return to the previous stage.

FIGURE 19
Completed Reading Lesson Plan: Emergent Reader (Stage 1)

Group: A   Date: 2-17-03

Rereading Level	Comments
1. Mary Had a Little Lamb 2. Big Sea Animals 2	most doing good - John still struggling
Word Bank Review Try to add the word "had"	Know these automatically Try to add new words
Word Study Alphabet Focus (Matching) BMSFA Concentration ✓ or Spell Check ✓	Recognize B, S, A - replace with 3 more letters tomorrow
Writing (Cut-Up Sentence) We had a big snow.	Spelled "We" and "had" without help
New Read Level 1. Playing Outside	

Conclusion

Traditional reading instruction often discourages guided contextual reading until students have mastered basic alphabet and phonemic awareness skills. Educators should not leave basic skills acquisition to chance; these skills should be included in carefully structured reading lessons for emergent readers. In these small instructional groups, teachers easily can assess and assist students with these skills. In addition, all students probably do not need a "letter-of-the-week" lesson in kindergarten. It is far more helpful to concentrate on letters students do *not* know. What about those 5-year-olds who already recognize the alphabet or even begin school as readers? If we are serious about increasing student achievement, these students should proceed to the next stage in their literacy development rather than review what they already know.

Emergent readers deal with unique challenges such as recognizing and producing letters, learning to track print, and acquiring a few sight words. These are critical understandings and are not to be underestimated. As teachers, we are laying the conceptual groundwork for the beginning reading process. No matter what grade a student is in, if he or she is an emergent reader, someone must take the time to lay the foundation for literacy success.

There is one word of caution in implementing reading groups for young children: Keep the lessons short and interactive—always keeping in mind that challenging yet achievable activities are critical. The fast-paced lessons that are presented in this book should keep all students interested.

CHAPTER 5

Stage 2: Beginning Reader

Characteristics of Beginning Readers

Beginning readers are starting to develop print-related understandings that underpin learning to read. They recognize and produce at least one half the alphabet and understand the concept of a word. After a simple sentence is read and finger pointed by the teacher, beginning readers can replicate the process. Additionally, these students are beginning to attend to initial sounds in words, though they may not yet identify all the letter names that go with the sounds. Beginning to recognize a few basic sight words in isolation is another characteristic of beginning readers. Clearly seeing printed words as units in text with recognizable beginning letters also characterizes beginning readers.

Texts for Beginning Readers

In the Beginning Reader stage, short, leveled books are the texts of choice. Look for books that have at least one or two lines of print per page. Picture books that use only one or two words for identification purposes are not appropriate. Students need practice in tracking lines of print. Books at this level should repeat sentence patterns and include picture support. Another element that can be helpful to beginning readers is rhyme. Finally, the repetition of high-frequency words in stories will help students build the word bank. The following book levels are appropriate for beginning readers:

Leveling System	Book Levels
Reading Recovery	3–5
DRA	3–5
Fountas and Pinnell	C–D

Instructional Strategies in the Beginning Reader Lesson Plan

Rereading

Day 1

- Echo read the first page or two to get students started. Provide enough support to get the children started and then let them take over. If you continue to echo read each page, the students may fail to progress.

FIGURE 20
Reading Lesson Plan: Beginning Reader (Stage 2)

Group:______________________________ Date:____________

Rereading Level	Comments
1.________________ 2.________________	
Word Bank	
Word Study Alphabet Focus __________ Picture Sorting__________ Concentration__________ or Spell Check__________	
Writing (Cut-Up Sentence) ________________	
New Read Level 1.________________	

Small-Group Reading Instruction: A Differentiated Teaching Model for Beginning and Struggling Readers by Beverly Tyner © 2003. Newark, DE: International Reading Association. May be copied for classroom use.

- Choral read by groups (girls read/boys read). Alternate choral reading and calling on individual students to read orally.
- When the book is completed, point to a few basic sight words to see if the students recognize them automatically. If they do, copy them on index cards and add them to the word bank. If they do not recognize them, try pointing to them at a later time so they can be added to the word bank.

Teacher: Yesterday we read a book called *A Friend for Little White Rabbit* (Randell, 1994a). Do you remember some of the animals that would not be friends when the white rabbit asks them to play?

Laura: There is a lamb and a duck.

Teacher: That's right. Which animal finally agrees to be a friend to the little white rabbit?

Harrison: The brown rabbit.

Teacher: Why do you think that the brown rabbit agrees to be the white rabbit's friend when the other animals would not play with the white rabbit?

Tommy: Because they are both rabbits.

(Teacher distributes individual copies of book to students.)

Teacher: Please remember to keep your books flat on the table. Let's read the title of the book together.

Students: *A Friend for Little White Rabbit.*

Teacher: Now let's turn to the first page. I'll read the first page to get us started and you follow along. (Teacher reads first page.) Now let's read this page together. (Choral read.)

Teacher: Turn to page 4. Girls, will you read this page that tells us what the little white lamb says?

Girls: "No, I will not," said the little white lamb. "Go away."

Teacher: Good job. The lamb is not being very nice to the rabbit. How do you think the rabbit is feeling?

Laura: I think it makes him feel sad.

Teacher: Let's turn to the next page on which we see the duck. Boys, will you read this page while the girls follow along with their fingers?

Boys: "Little white duck, little white duck, please will you play with me?" said the little white rabbit.

(The book is completed with variations of choral reading and calling on individual students. The teacher asks questions concerning the story to enhance comprehension.)

Teacher: Do you think that the white rabbit will ever ask any other animals besides rabbits to play with him?

Catherine: No. He knows they won't play with him.

Teacher: Does anyone think that he will?

Beth: Yes, I do. Maybe they will be nice next time.

(Teacher takes up the books.) Let's go back in this book and look at a new word. (Teacher points to the word *look*.) What's this word?

Students: *Look*.

Teacher: Let's add this word to our word bank. I'll write it on this card while you spell it for me.

Teacher: You really did a great job reading that book. We will read it again tomorrow. I'll leave a copy of it in the book center for you to practice reading.

Day 2

Several strategies can be used as students reread text including partner reading, group oral reading, or individual oral reading.

- Have students read with a partner (alternating pages) as you observe, helping as needed. If there are an odd number of students, you may act as a partner.
- Have students read aloud independently while you observe. Encourage students to whisper read or try using a PVC pipe as a reading telephone (see Figure 21). It allows students to hear themselves read clearly even when they whisper and to focus without hearing others read.

FIGURE 21
Students Whisper Read Using PVC Pipes as Reading Telephones

- Have individual students read orally while the rest of the group follows along. I have found that children enjoy oral reading when they can confidently read instructionally appropriate text. In a small group in which everyone gets a frequent turn, oral reading is enjoyed and supported as students develop fluency. Just make sure that you mix up your oral reading strategies and never call on students to read in a systematic way in which students predict their turns and become disinterested.

Teacher: (Holding up cover of the book *Baby Panda* [Randell, 2000]) Who remembers the name of this kind of bear?

Nick: Panda.

Teacher: Yes. It is a baby panda.

(Teacher distributes copies of the book.)

Teacher: You are going to read this book with a partner today. Remember, when you partner read, you take turns reading the pages with your partner. If your partner needs help, you can help him or her with a word. If you both need help, just look at me and I will help you. Remember to read softly but loud enough for your partner to hear you. When you are ready, you may begin reading the book with your partner.

(Teacher monitors as students complete the book reading.)

Teacher: I'll put this in your book box in the book center so you can read this book by yourselves.

LITERACY CENTER ALERT

Provide a basket of "reading telephones" in the book center. They help keep the noise level down and the students focused. Also, place books used during rereading in the book center for independent reading.

Word Bank

- Continue to look in the books for new words that most of the group recognizes to add to the word bank.
- Flash the words quickly to the group or individuals (see Figure 22).
- Continue to build the group word bank to 20. When the group reaches 20, keep 5 words and retire the others to the word work center. Never have more than 20 words in the word bank because it is too time-consuming to continue to review them.
- Continue to fill in Watch Our Sight Words Grow (see Appendix D, p. 239).

FIGURE 22
A Teacher Flashes Word Bank Words to a Student

Teacher:	Your word bank has really been growing. You already have 18 words. Let's quickly flash through your word bank cards and see how quickly you can say them. (Teacher first flashes cards for group responses and then goes around the circle for individual responses.)

LITERACY CENTER ALERT

Play "Beat the Clock" using the retired word bank words. All you need is a timer. Let students see how quickly they can recognize 20 or more words. Each student could keep a record of his or her best time for fun.

Word Study

Alphabet Focus

- Complete the word study (alphabet recognition started in Stage 1). Additionally, begin consonant picture sorts using the picture cards in Appendix B (pp. 135–149).
- Begin with the picture cards for the letters *b*, *s*, and *m*, and continue with the consonant sequence suggested—BSM, CFD, TRL, NPW, GHJ, ZKV. Consonants are presented in sets of three. The sets are chosen based on their distinct sounds.
- Always use the same pictures as the header cards at the top of each column so that there is always a "known" picture card for reference.

Whereas some children have little difficulty with phonemic awareness (being able to distinguish sounds), others find the task difficult and need time to develop this important strategy. The process used to introduce this strategy is critical to student success.

Picture Sorting

On the first day of the sort, go through all the pictures to make sure that students can identify each picture name (don't use pictures that continually confuse the group).

- Remember, the sort is by the beginning sound, not the letter name.
- Usually, sort three picture cards across and four down:

Header Cards →

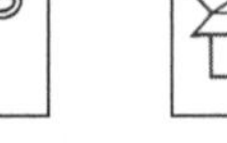

- Taking turns, give each child a picture card to sort in the appropriate column. Ask where each picture goes. After the card has been placed, ask the whole group to read the picture cards in the column as they listen for the correct beginning sound.
- After completing the sort, you will either (a) turn the cards over and play Concentration or (b) Spell Check using the remaining alphabet letters you are working on or, if the alphabet is complete, use the picture cards and ask students to write the beginning sounds.
- As the children begin to sort the pictures by beginning sound with confidence, they are ready for the next step—sorting the picture against the letter.
- Begin by placing the three header cards with a letter card above each picture:

Pointing to the first picture card, explain,

> If we were to write the word *bird*, the first letter would be a *b*. The letter *b* stands for the first sound we hear in *bird*. The *s* stands for the first sound we hear in *sun*, and *m* is the letter that stands for the first sound we hear in *man*. Now let's sort these pictures under the right letter cards.

- The picture card is taken away after each match to make sure the students are not relying on the pictures for clues.
- As the students become accurate and confident in manipulating the consonant sounds for *b*, *s*, and *m*, the next three consonants (*c*, *f*, *d*) can be introduced. The students' learning rate will usually be faster on the second set of consonants. There is no need to rush; make sure that the students are making accurate, fluent responses before moving on.

Teacher: We are going to listen for words that begin with the same sound. All the picture names begin with the same sound as *bird*, *sun*, or *man* (point to header cards). We are going to put the picture cards in the correct columns. Watch, I'll do the first one.

(The teacher picks up the picture card *box* and places it under *bird* and pronounces both words, emphasizing the beginning sound.)

Teacher: *Box* goes under *bird* because they begin with the same sound. Now you do the next one.

(One student has difficulty with his attempt.)

Teacher: Listen: *monkey—bird.* These two words do not have the same beginning sound.

(Then, the teacher moves *monkey* into the correct column, under *man*, and pronounces both words. The students take turns sorting the picture cards by beginning consonant sounds. Each time a card is sorted in a particular column, the students read all the words in that column [starting at the top] to determine whether they begin with the same sound.)

Concentration

Follow the Concentration directions in chapter 4, p. 56. This game will be played in the same manner as in Stage 1, but instead of looking for letter matches, students will be looking for picture cards that begin with the same sound.

Teacher: Now that we have finished sorting our picture cards, let's turn the cards over for a quick game of Concentration. (Teacher turns cards over and mixes them up.)

Teacher: John, you may go first. (Student turns over bird picture.) John, what is that a picture of?

John: A bird.

Teacher: What sound do you hear at the beginning of *bird*?

John: Bird. *B*. It starts with a *b*.

Teacher: Now turn over another card, and see if you can find another picture that begins with that same sound.

(John turns over star picture card.)

Teacher: What sound do you hear at the beginning of *star*?

John: Star. *S*. I hear an *s* sound.

Teacher: Is that the same sound that you heard at the beginning of *bird*?

John: No.

Teacher: It's not a match so we will turn them back over. Remember to look at the cards carefully so that you will know where they are when it is your turn.

(Game is completed when all matches are made. When students make a match, they get an extra turn. The student with the most matches at the end of the game is the winner.)

Spell Check

After students complete alphabet recognition and production in word study, they are ready to move to Spell Check with beginning sounds. Spell Check requires students to write the beginning sound they hear in the picture cards.

- As students become accurate in writing the beginning sound in a word, begin asking for the ending consonant sound. (Make sure these words have definite consonant endings because if you ask for the ending sound for *baby*, students might become confused.)
- Have students complete the Spell Check in their student journals.
- Never use more than five words for Spell Check.
- Check each letter sound together as students complete the task.

Note: Sort the picture cards every day, and rotate between Concentration and Spell Check. Usually there will not be time for both.

Teacher: Let's write some of the letters that represent the sounds that we are working on. (Teacher hands out pencils and paper that have been numbered from one to five.)

Teacher: Put your finger beside number one. Write the letter sound that you hear at the beginning of *bird*.

(Students write, and teacher assists individual students if they are having difficulty.)

Teacher: (Holding up the *b* letter card) Did everyone write the letter *b*? If you wrote the letter *b*, give yourself a check (✓).

Spell Check is completed after five words are given. The teacher also may ask more advanced students to write the ending consonant sounds.

Writing

Continue to use the process for writing outlined in Stage 1 (see chapter 4, p. 60). Now, the sentences will contain some words that begin with the consonant letters being studied. High-frequency words also are included from the word bank.

- At the conclusion of the group cut-up sentence, give each student an individual cut-up sentence (the same as the group sentence) to be pasted in the correct order in his or her journal.
- After the first few days, the pasted cut-up sentence in the journal becomes an independent activity. Also, ask students to draw a picture to accompany the sentence (see Figure 23).

FIGURE 23
Student Sample of a Pasted Cut-Up Sentence and Drawing

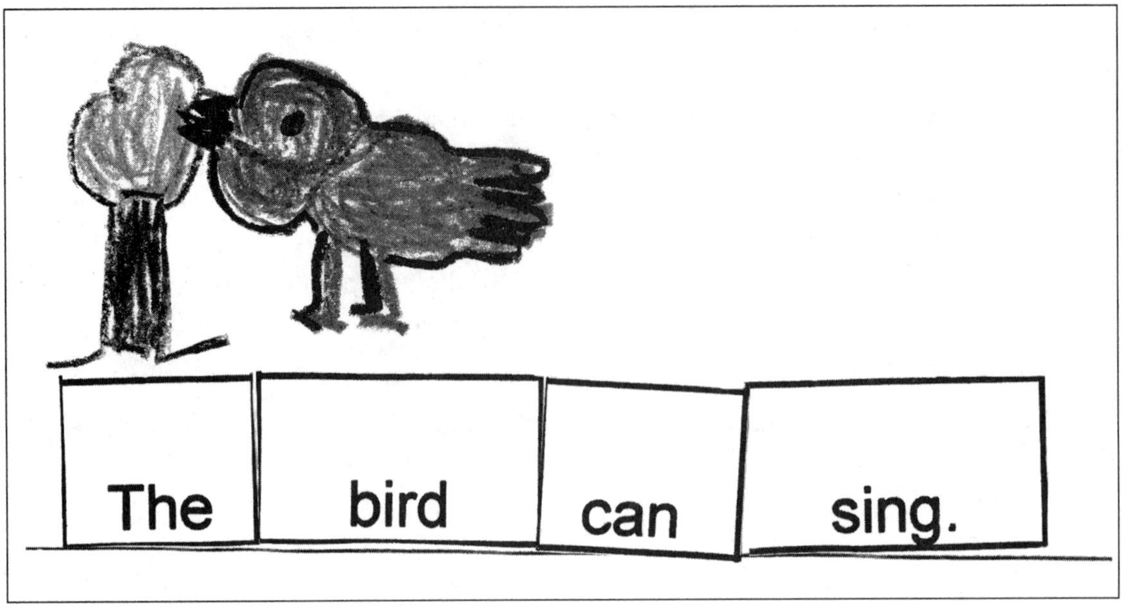

The bird can sing.

Teacher: Because we have read several books about rabbits, or "bunnies," we are going to write a sentence about them. Listen: *The little bunny is soft.* (This sentence is selected because it has several word bank words and two words that have beginning sounds that are the focus in word study.)

Teacher: (Teacher points to fingers in a left-to-right progression as students watch.) Listen again: *The little bunny is soft.*

Teacher: Now hold up your left hand, and point to your fingers while we say this sentence together.

Students: The little bunny is soft.

Teacher: How many words do we have in our sentence today?

Students: Five.

Teacher: (Writing on sentence strip as students watch) What is the first word in our sentence?

Beth: The.

Teacher: Yes. *The* is the first word and it is one of our word bank words. Who remembers how to spell the word *the*?

Andy: T-h-e.

Teacher: What kind of letter should we use at the beginning of a sentence?

Jill: A capital letter.

Teacher:	Yes, we always start a sentence with a capital letter. Let's leave two finger spaces before we write our next word. What word comes next?
Nick:	Little.
Teacher:	Yes, *little*. How does *little* sound at the beginning?
Jill:	L.
Teacher:	Yes, and that sound is represented by the letter *l*. I will write the rest of the word, and you tell me the letters. (Students name letters as teacher writes the word *little*.)

The sentence writing is completed as you guide the discussion emphasizing letter names and sounds that are currently being studied. In addition, spacing between words and punctuation is discussed. The sentence is then cut into individual words and distributed to the group. The cut-up sentence is then reconstructed and placed in a plastic bag in the word work center for later use.

(For examples of cut-up sentences for each group of consonants, see Appendix C, pp. 224–229.)

Note: Ten sample sentences are provided for each set of consonants. Remain on the set until the group is confident, and then move on. Few students will need to go through all the sentences.

LITERACY CENTER ALERT

The cut-up sentence journals serve as excellent practice reading for beginning readers. Store them in the book center, and students will have materials they can read.

New Read

- Introduce the book by conducting a picture walk using your book. Encourage students to look at the pictures while you verbalize the story. Build background knowledge if necessary, and make predictions based on the picture walk.
- Distribute student books.
- Begin reading, and let the students join with you in choral reading as quickly as possible.
- Alternate echo reading, choral reading, and independent reading until the story is completed.

Teacher:	Let's take a look at our new book today. (Teacher holds up the front cover of the book and does not give out individual book copies.) The title of the book is *Monkey on the Roof* (Clough, 2000). Does that look like a real monkey?
Paul:	No, it doesn't.

Teacher: I wonder how that monkey got on the roof?

Helen: The boy threw it up there.

Teacher: Let's take a look at the pictures in this story to see if we can find out. This is Matthew, and this is Emma (teacher points to the pictures). What are they doing with the monkey?

Katie: Playing a game with it.

Teacher: Oh, no. Now I see how the monkey got on the roof. Do you think that Mom knows yet? Let's turn the page. What are the children doing in this picture?

Clint: Telling Mom.

Teacher: I wonder how they will get the monkey down. What do you think?

Paul: They could climb out the window.

Helen: They could get a ladder.

(The picture walk continues as the teacher leads students in predicting and confirming based on picture illustrations. The teacher stops on the next to last page.)

Teacher: Do you think they will ever play that game again? Let's read the story and find out.

(Teacher distributes individual books to students or may choose to hold the book and let the group read along from her copy, especially if time is running short.)

Teacher: Look at page 3. I will read this page first, and you follow along. (The teacher reads a page.) Now I want you to read the page with me. Ready?

Teacher and Students: "Look," said Matthew. "Look at Monkey!" "Up he goes," said Emma.

Teacher: Turn the page, please. You know most of the words on this page, and I think you can read it without my help. Who would like to read this page for us? (Student volunteers.)

Paul: "Oh!" said Emma. "Look at the Monkey! He is up on the roof."

Teacher: You did a great job. Did anyone notice those marks around the words that Emma is saying on that page? Those are called *quotation marks*, and they show us the exact words that Emma said. Let's go back and read that page together, and try to make it sound like Emma really says those words.

(The first read of the book is completed as individual students or groups of students participate in the reading. After the book is completed, the teacher goes back to the text to find specific words that might be added to the group word bank.)

See Figure 24 for a completed lesson plan for beginning readers.

FIGURE 24
Completed Reading Lesson Plan: Beginning Reader (Stage 2)

Group: B　　Date: March 3, 2003

Rereading Level	Comments
1. A Friend for Little White Rabbit - 5 2. Baby Panda - 5	Good rereads. Anna still struggling
Word Bank Add "look"	
Word Study Alphabet Focus (Completed) Picture Sorting BSM Concentration ✓ or Spell Check ✓	Ready for next letters: CFD
Writing (Cut-Up Sentence) The little bunny is soft.	Start tomorrow with individual cut up sentence in student journal (at work table)
New Read Level 1. Monkey on the Roof 5	

When to Move to the Next Stage

Several skills should be mastered before students are ready to begin the Fledgling Reader stage. Along with complete alphabet recognition and production, students should be able to identify beginning and ending sounds in words. Many students may still confuse several letters (e.g., *y* and *w*), but this is perfectly normal. Additionally, before moving to Stage 3, students should be able to quickly identify at least 20 sight words from the word bank. They also should be fluent and confident in finger-point reading simple texts. When making the decision to move to the next stage, look at the overall progress of the group. Remember that students will continue to review beginning and ending sounds in the context of words instead of pictures in the next phase of word study. As previously stated, it is better to make the mistake of moving ahead too quickly than to remain in material that is not challenging to students.

Conclusion

The beginning reader is like a sitting rocket being fueled. These readers are now equipped with the basic strategies that will launch them into the world of reading. It is in this Beginning Reader stage that many slower learners and ESL students need extra time. The diligent work done with the beginning reader is well worth the effort. The next stage, Fledgling Reader, is one of great excitement for both students and teachers.

CHAPTER 6

Stage 3: Fledgling Reader

Characteristics of Fledgling Readers

For teachers who have carefully laid the foundation, the work in the previous stages is fully realized in the Fledgling Reader stage. Fledgling readers, although inexperienced, are equipped with the knowledge necessary to begin decoding and comprehension processes. Additionally, these students can quickly and automatically recognize approximately 50 basic sight words. Fledgling readers can easily read text with simple sentence structure and significant picture support. Major focuses for the fledgling reader are systematically studying short-vowel word families, developing a more extensive sight vocabulary, and reading more complex text. Students also will begin to use self-correction as a reading strategy.

Texts for Fledgling Readers

Using carefully leveled books is critical for success in early reading. For fledgling readers, choose texts that contain a variety of sentence patterns and punctuation. Partially patterned text with moderate picture support should be considered. Books that contain high-frequency words, as well as easily decodable words, are also important in text selection. The following are appropriate book levels for fledgling readers:

Leveling System	Book Levels
Reading Recovery	6–11
DRA	6–10
Fountas and Pinnell	E–G

Instructional Strategies in the Fledgling Reader Lesson Plan

Rereading

As students progress to longer books, there may be time for only one reread.

- Reread yesterday's new read using varied strategies such as choral or individual reading.
- The reread could be done as a partner read or with the reading telephones so that everyone rereads the entire text.

FIGURE 25

Reading Lesson Plan: Fledgling Reader (Stage 3)

Group:______________________________ Date:______________

Rereading Level	Comments
1.______________________	
Word Bank	
Word Study Word Family Sort______________ Concentration______________ or Spell Check______________ or Word Scramble______________	
Writing (Sentence Dictation)	
New Read Level 1.______________________	

Teacher: Yesterday we read the book *Honey for Baby Bear* (Randell, 1994b). Today we are going to read the book again, but this time you are going to whisper read using your reading telephones. (Teacher distributes individual books and PVC pipe telephones.) You may begin reading, but remember to read loud enough so I can hear you. What are some things you can do on your own if you come to a word that you don't know?

Laura: You can look at the beginning sound.

Paul: You can think of a word that makes sense.

Teacher: If you still need help, just look at me and I will help you.

(The teacher observes and monitors as students read the book. The teacher listens in as students read, assisting when necessary. After everyone is finished, the teacher collects the books, and then he or she may choose to return to the text to search for words that can be added to the group word bank.)

Note: An in-depth discussion to enhance comprehension was conducted the previous day so that very little time is spent in discussion with the reread. The purposes for the reread are to practice reading simple text and to develop fluency.

Word Bank

Continue to look in the books read for new words to add to the word bank. You also may add two words to the word bank from each word family being studied. Flash the word bank words to the group or to individuals.

Optional Game for Word Bank

This game is called Not. Simply add several word cards printed with the word *not* to the word bank. Quickly flash the word bank cards to individual students, allowing the students to keep the words they identify correctly. If the word *not* appears at a student's turn, he or she must return all cards to you. Set a timer for three minutes. When the timer goes off, the game is over. The student with the most cards at the end of the game wins.

Word Study

Word study for the fledgling reader involves systematic study of short-vowel word families, beginning with the *A* family. Remember, this is also a good review for beginning- and ending-consonant letter sounds. Even if you are working with low-level readers, they should begin the *A* family as quickly as possible.

This phase of word study will be long and important. It will involve (a) sorting short-vowel words into rhyming categories (*cat, mat* and *wig, pig*), (b) committing a good number of these words to sight memory, and (c) developing competence in spelling these patterns.

FIGURE 26
Students Involved in a Word Family Sort

Word Family Sort

Begin with the first three header cards for the *A* family: *cat*, *man*, and *cap* (see Figure 26). These should be three words that the students recognize, or you can add a picture with the header card for more support.

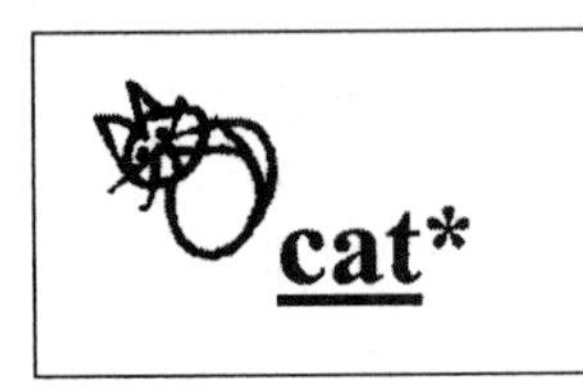

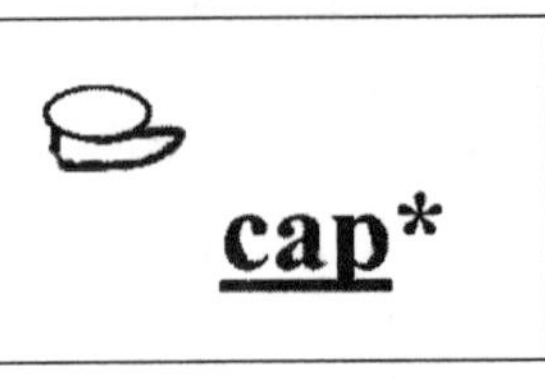

- Demonstrate the process to the students. For example, start with the word card *mat*. Ask the students in which column the word should be placed. Slide the card under each word and then place it under *cat*. Never require students to say the word first, and then sort it. If students know the header card and sort the word correctly, they can identify the new word by substituting the beginning sound.
- Continue to take turns, allowing the students to sort the cards in the appropriate column. After each card has been moved to a column, have the students start with the top header card and read the words in the column to determine if they are placed correctly.
- Use three cards across the top and four down. This activity will be fast paced to allow time to complete the other lesson components. Notice that a word containing a blend is included as the last word in the column. This allows students to practice the three-letter (consonant-vowel-consonant) words before adding a more complex pattern (consonant-consonant-vowel-consonant).

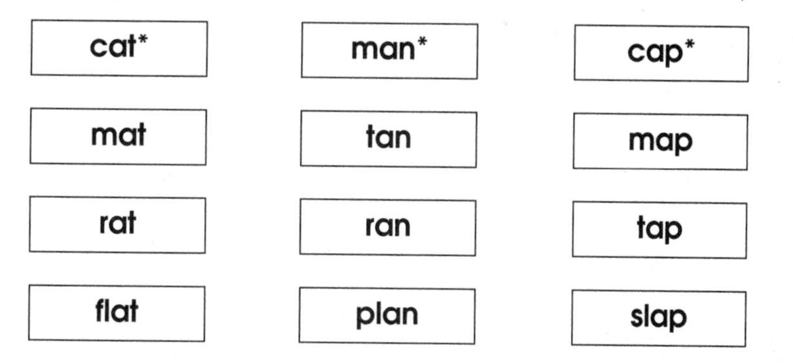

- When the students can confidently and automatically recognize the words when mixed, substitute a fourth pattern (*ack* pattern) for one of the other header words.
- The first pattern studied, the *A* family, is challenging for most students, so plan to spend extended time in this part of word study. If you are working with more challenged students, start with sorting two families or restrict the sorting to the three-letter words.
- When the group has successfully mastered the *A* family, move to the *I* family and follow the same process. The three header cards for the *I* family are *hit*, *win*, and *big*:

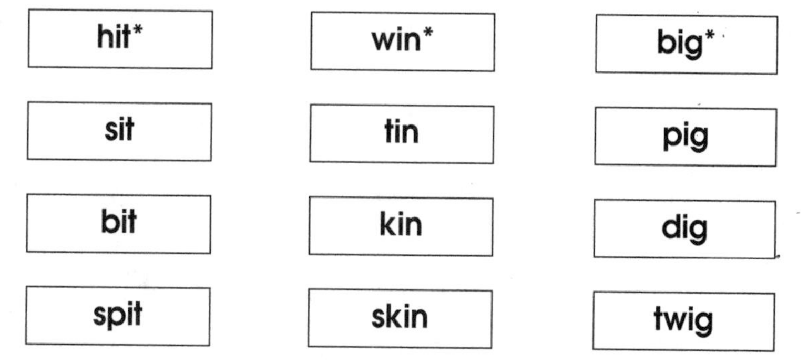

- When the students become confident with these three patterns, add the *ick* pattern to replace one of the other families.
- After mastering the *A* and *I* word families, review the patterns by mixing the two families. This exercise ensures that students can clearly distinguish between the short *a* and short *i* sounds. Although there are a variety of combinations for *a* and *i*, remember to use only three or four header cards across the top. For example, *man-big-cat*.
- Spend as much time as necessary with this mix before moving ahead.
- Then, move to the *O* family. Following the established routines, complete the *O* family word study.
- Review with the students by mixing the *A*, *I*, and *O* families.
- Using this same routine, complete the *U* and *E* families.
- As the rhyming word families are completed, review short vowels in words without rhyming patterns. The following is the short-vowel sequence in word study:

Short-Vowel Word Families

1	2	3	4	5
a	i	o	u	e
-at	-it	-ot	-ut	-et
-an	-ig	-op	-ug	-ed
-ap	-in	-ob	-un	-en
-ack	-ick	-ock	-uck	-ell

Short-Vowel Patterns

a	i	o	u	e
b<u>a</u>d	p<u>i</u>g	m<u>o</u>m	b<u>u</u>s	p<u>e</u>t

Complete word study lists and cards are found in Appendix B (p. 132). Additionally, a concise Word Sort Instructions and Sequence can be found in Appendix D (p. 245). Establishing effective routines for word study is important for success in developing decoding skills.

Teacher: We finished the *O* family yesterday, so today we will review the *A*, *I*, and *O* families by combining them. These will be the four header cards for our sorting activity today: *cat*, *hit*, *mop*, *hot*. Let's read them together before we get started. (Students read with the teacher.)

Teacher: (Teacher hands first card, *sit*, to student.) Where would this word go? Remember, sort your card under the right word before you try to say it.

(The student correctly places the card under the word *hit*.)

Teacher: Thumbs up if you think the card is in the right place? Good. Now, let's read these two words together.

Brianna: *Hit. Sit.*

Teacher: How are these two words alike?

Brianna: They both have the short *i* sound.

Teacher: Yes, they both have the short vowel sound *i*.

(The sorting activity continues as students are given word cards to sort and read.)

Follow up the word sorting with one of the following activities: Concentration, Spell Check, or a new activity called Word Scramble.

Concentration

After completing the word sorting activity, turn over the cards and mix them up. Play Concentration by having students turn over cards to find word family matches. Limit the number of word cards if the game gets too long.

Spell Check

- Using the word study words, call out five words for students to write in their journals (see Figure 27).
- Check each word as it is completed by the group, and assist as needed.
- When Spell Check is completed, have students read aloud the five words.

Word Scramble

Make a set of alphabet letter cards for each group member (see Appendix B, pp. 133–134). Choose seven or eight letters for each student to use. The following is an example of Word Scramble for the *A* and *I* word families:

Distribute letter cards: h, o, t, b, i, s, p
Directions to students:

1. Make the word *hot*.
2. Change one letter to make the word *hit*.
3. Change one letter to make the word *bit*.
4. Change one letter to make the word *sit*.
5. Change one letter to make the word *pit*.
6. Add one letter to make the word *spit*.

Note: See Appendix C (pp. 204–223) for Word Scramble activities for each word family.

FIGURE 27
Spell Check Example
Mixing *A*, *I*, and *O*

Writing

Select a short sentence that incorporates some sight and word study words. (Examples for each vowel family are in Appendix C.)

- Tell students the sentence for the day. (For example, *The cat plays a lot of tricks.*) Repeat the sentence several times with the students, counting the number of words.
- Using a sentence strip, write the sentence as the students contribute. Ask who can spell the first word, what kind of letter it begins with, and what goes at the end of the sentence. Focus on the short-vowel sounds (*a*, *i*, *o*) that are a part of the word study.
- After completing the sentence, leave it posted and ask the students to write the same sentence in their journals. Tell the students to try to write the sentence by themselves, but if they need help, they can look at the sentence. Gradually, take away the sentence while the students complete the writing activity. This transitional writing activity helps students develop independence in using learned strategies and prepares them to write dictated sentences.

New Read

- End the lesson by introducing a new book and completing a picture walk with the first few pages. An entire picture walk of the book is not necessary.
- Continue to encourage students to make predictions and text connections.
- Distribute the books, and let the students read using a variety of strategies and with support only as needed.

- Echo reading should be limited to the beginning pages and hard parts.
- Encourage students to use beginning and ending sounds as well as short-vowel word knowledge to decode unknown words.

Teacher: Our new book today is *Brown Mouse Plays a Trick* (Giles, 2001). Let's take a look at the cover of the book. What kind of party do you think they are having?

Joan: A birthday party.

Teacher: What kind of trick do you think brown mouse will play?

Mary: Maybe he will pretend that he won't get a present.

Clint: Maybe he will hide when the party starts.

Teacher: Those are good guesses. Everyone turn to page 2, and we will read and find out. I will read this page to get us started while you follow along. (Teacher reads) Please turn the page. I want everyone to whisper read this page to find out why the mice can't go home.

(Using quiet voices, the students each read the page while the teacher observes.)

Teacher: Now find the sentence that tells us why the mice can't go home. Frank, please read that sentence for us.

Frank: Brown Mouse went to the door and looked out. "You can't go home," he said. "The cat is outside the door."

Teacher: Remember the cover of the book? Does anyone want to change his or her prediction about the trick?

Mary: He is going to trick the cat.

Teacher: Mary, will you read the next page for us to see how the mice might get home?

Mary: "I will make my toy mouse run outside," said Brown Mouse. "The cat will run after it, and you can get home."

Teacher: Do you think Brown Mouse has a good idea?

Clint: Yes. He is really tricky.

(The book is completed using a variety of reading strategies focusing on decoding and comprehension.)

LITERACY CENTER ALERT

When the lesson is completed, take the new read to the book center and place it in the group's reading box so the students can reread it individually or with a partner.

See Figure 28 for a completed lesson plan for fledgling readers.

FIGURE 28

Completed Reading Lesson Plan: Fledgling Reader (Stage 3)

Group: C   Date: November 12, 2002

	Comments
Rereading Level 1. Honey for Baby Bear 9	Good reread
Word Bank Review- Play the game "not"	Know these automatically - send 15 to word study center - add new words
Word Study Word Family Sort a-o-i Concentration ✓ or Spell Check ✓ or Word Scramble ✓	Sort cat hit mop hot
Writing (Sentence Dictation) The cat plays a lot of tricks.	John needed some help - still struggling with short i
New Read Level 1. Brown Mouse Plays a Trick - 9	Little challenge - Start 10's on Monday.

When to Move to the Next Stage

There are several milestones to consider prior to advancing to the Transitional Reader stage. First, students should be able to automatically recognize many short-vowel words. Students also should be able to recognize at least 100 sight words. At this point, completion of a quick Reading Review is feasible to determine if students are reading at an appropriate instructional level (see details in chapter 2). This assessment should provide ample information for determining readiness for the next reading stage as well as readiness to advance in word study.

Conclusion

The Fledgling Reader stage allows students to improve and extend their existing range of skills. By combining their knowledge of prior experiences, sounds, writing, and story structure, fledgling readers are bringing meaning to their reading. These students exhibit greater confidence as readers and are capable of reading and enjoying more complex stories. The next stage, Transitional Reader, advances the reader toward independence.

CHAPTER 7

Stage 4: Transitional Reader

Characteristics of Transitional Readers

Although they still rely on teacher support, transitional readers are working toward reading independence. These readers have a basic sight word vocabulary of at least 100 words. Additionally, these readers can confidently read one-syllable, short-vowel words using consonant blends and digraphs. Whereas learning to read and process text has been the primary focus for emergent, beginning, and fledgling readers, there is a shift for transitional readers to orchestrate decoding and comprehension strategies. Word study moves to one-syllable vowel patterns (for example, short, long, and r-controlled). Finally, developing reading fluency plays an important role in the transitional reader stage.

Texts for Transitional Readers

The leveled texts used for the transitional reader should include longer stories with less emphasis on sentence patterns, which support the reader. Stories also will include some unfamiliar or specialized vocabulary, especially in nonfiction selections. These texts will rely less on illustrations as clues to make meaning in context. In selecting texts for transitional readers, consider stories that allow students opportunities to practice integrating the cueing systems that answer the following questions: Does it look right? Does it sound right? Does it make sense? The following are appropriate book levels for transitional readers:

Leveling System	Book Levels
Reading Recovery	12–16
DRA	11–17
Fountas and Pinnell	H–I

Instructional Strategies in the Transitional Reader Lesson Plan

Rereading

Rereading plays an important role in developing reading fluency. Although transitional readers can read the text accurately, they may be rather slow and choppy at doing so. One way to address this concern is for you to be a part of the rereading process by alternating turns with the students. Your oral reading provides a fluent model for the

FIGURE 29
Reading Lesson Plan: Transitional Reader (Stage 4)

Group: ______________________________ Date: ______________

Rereading Level	Comments
1.______________________	
Word Bank	
Word Study Vowel Pattern Sort______________ Vowel Pattern Concentration__________ or Spell Check________________ or Word Scramble______________	
Writing (Sentence Dictation) ______________________ ______________________	
New Read Level 1.______________________	

students to emulate. These readers can benefit significantly from listening to and visually following along with you. Another technique involves reading a page and then asking students to read the same page to see if they can emulate you. Rereading can be conducted using these techniques, along with those mentioned previously, such as partner or individual reading.

Teacher: (Distributing books) Yesterday we read the book *Jessica in the Dark* (Randell, 1997b). Think about the story and its events. I would like for someone to summarize this story for us. Remember to include the setting, main characters, problem, and solution in your summary.

Katherine: Well, it is raining at Jessica's house, and her brother Daniel leaves his favorite toy outside in the tree house. It is dark, but Jessica wants to get it anyway. She is a little bit scared. Daniel is happy when she brings Rex back.

Teacher: Thank you. In less than 30 seconds, you gave us a summary that included all the main points. Now I want you to reread this book with your reading partner, alternating pages. If you need help and your partner can't help you, look at me and I will help. You may begin reading.

(The teacher monitors as students complete books.)

Word Bank

Keep building the word bank by continuing the same process used in Stages 1–3. Keep notes on commonly missed sight words in oral reading, and add those words to the word bank. After 100 words (or 5 sets of 20), you may modify the word bank to include specialized vocabulary or tricky words found in the stories.

Word Study

Now transitional readers are ready to study another important aspect of word recognition—the teaching of high-frequency, one-syllable vowel patterns. Success in mastering vowel patterns depends on previous success in mastering consonant sounds, word families, and short vowels. For example, mastery of beginning consonants prepares students for short-vowel word family sorts. Success in reading and spelling the short vowels naturally leads into work on the five short-vowel patterns, and mastery of the short-vowel words brings essential knowledge to the one-syllable vowel pattern stage. The sequence for word study in vowel patterns Level 1 is shown here:

a	i	o	u	e
cat	hid	mom	mud	red
make	ride	rope	cute	feet
car	girl	for	hurt	her
day		go	blue	he
		boat		
		look		
		cow		

Vowel Pattern Sort

The word sorting technique used with word families lends itself nicely to work with vowel patterns. The word study in vowel patterns begins by sorting each vowel pattern beginning with *A* pattern words in Level 1.

- Begin by placing the first three header cards on the table: *cat*, *make*, and *car*.
- Model the task by showing students that each of the words goes in one of the columns (see Figure 30). Remind students that they must not only look at the words but also listen for the sound *a* makes in each word: *bad, same, hard.*
- Students sort 15 words with you modeling the correct response if necessary.
- As students gain confidence and accuracy with these three patterns, a fourth pattern can be added (*ay* pattern): *mat, make, car, day.*

As a way to keep all students actively involved, the sorting activity can be turned into a game.

- Students take turns sorting one word at a time, then reading the column of words.
- If a student sorts the words and reads the column correctly, he or she receives 2 points (1 for sorting and 1 for reading).
- If a student identifies another student sorting incorrectly, he or she receives a point.
- The player with the most points at the end of the game wins.

An advantage of this game is that all students are involved and paying attention; they love the competition. Follow up the sorting activity with one of the following activities: Vowel Pattern Concentration, Spell Check, or Word Scramble.

FIGURE 30
A Student Participates in a Vowel Pattern Sort

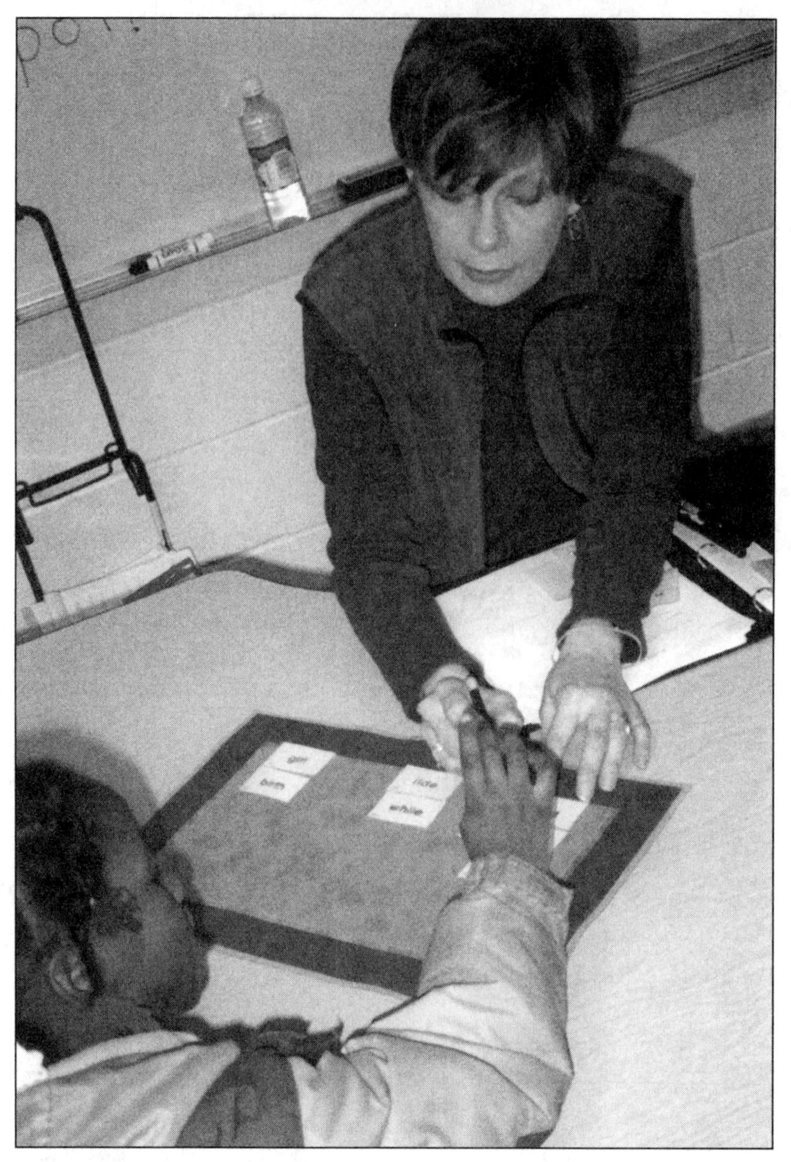

Vowel Pattern Concentration

- After the sort is completed, quickly turn over the cards and mix them up.
- Taking turns, each player turns over two word cards. If the cards are a pattern match (*rake–same*), the student reads and keeps the cards. The student also gets another turn. If the cards do not match, the player must read them and turn them face down.
- The game is over when all word cards have been removed from the board. The player finding the most word pattern matches is the winner.

Spell Check

- Select 5 words from the *A* pattern study.
- Call out each word, and have the students write the words in their journals.
- Together, check the words.

Word Scramble

This activity enhances the students' abilities to see relationships among words.

- Choose 8–10 of the same letters for each student to work with.
- Ask students to make each word as you say it.
- Together, check each word before moving on to the next word.

Word Scramble Sample Activity: *A* Patterns

Letter cards:

1. Make the word *cake*.

2. Change one letter to make *lake*.

3. Change two letters to make the word *race*.

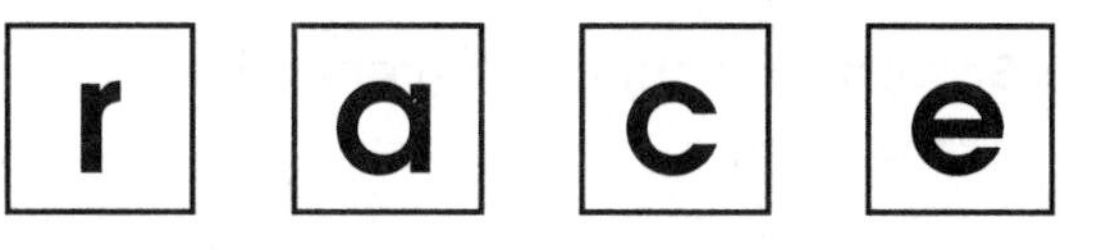

4. Add one letter to make the word *trace*.

t r a c e

See Appendix C for sample Word Scramble activities for each vowel pattern (pp. 204–223).

As a culminating activity, when you feel that the group is ready to move on, timed trials can be used to increase students' automaticity in recognizing word patterns.

- Set a timer for one minute.
- Shuffle a deck of cards containing all *A* pattern words listed in Level 1 (see Appendix B).
- Give each student one minute to read correctly as many words as possible.
- At the end of one minute, count the number of words in the correct pile.
- The student who recognized the most words in one minute is the winner.

This activity will serve as an excellent assessment in determining the group's readiness to proceed to the next vowel pattern.

Teachers sometimes become frustrated when students are unable to transfer their word study skills into real reading and writing. It is critical that you point out words in stories that contain word patterns. Additionally, you should call attention to word patterns in teacher- or student-generated writing.

Writing

Sentence dictation for students at this level is quick and straightforward. The goal is to provide students with an opportunity to use word patterns in writing complete sentences.

- Use the suggested sentences in Appendix C (pp. 230–237), or make up your own sentences that incorporate the focus vowel pattern words.
- Repeat the sentence several times, and then ask the students to repeat the sentence with you.
- As the students write the sentence (see Figure 31), assist any student who is having difficulty.
- When the students are finished, write the sentence on the board or a sentence strip so that the students can self-correct their errors.

FIGURE 31
Student Example of Sentence Dictation

Dad made a trap for the shark.

Teacher: Our sentence today is *Dad made a trap for the shark.* Listen again: *Dad made a trap for the shark.* Now say the sentence with me.

Teacher and Students: *Dad made a trap for the shark.*

Teacher: Now pick up your pencils, and write the sentence.

(Students begin writing.)

Teacher: (reaches over to assist a child) Lauren, do you remember the *a* pattern in the word *shark*?

Lauren: Is it "ar"?

Teacher: Yes, it is. Good for you. Now I'll write the sentence on the board so that you can check your work.

New Read

The new read will provide students with an opportunity to develop comprehension skills.

- Before reading the story, ask students to make a prediction about the story's content based only on the title and the front cover.
- Picture walk the first several pages only.
- Begin reading the book. After reading several pages, ask students if they want to keep or modify their predictions and to explain why.
- At strategic points in the story (three or four times), stop to ask questions about what is happening so far (summarizing), what students think will happen (predicting), and what students remember (recalling).

It is important that the new read be done with all students reading and contributing to the discussion to achieve maximum success with both reading and comprehension development.

Teacher: Our new book today is about some animals. Look at the cover. Do you know what kind of animals these are?

Beth: Beavers.

Teacher: Yes, these are beavers. The name of our book is *The Busy Beavers* (Randell, 1997a). What do you know about beavers?

Ed: They have big teeth and chew wood.

Teacher: Yes, they do. Have you ever seen a beaver? (Teacher tries to make text connections for students. If the teacher feels that the background knowledge is still lacking, he or she may choose to build more background knowledge before continuing.)

Teacher: Do you think this book will be fiction or nonfiction?

Jill: I think it will be nonfiction because the beavers look real.

Teacher: Let's all turn to page 2. I will read the first page to get us started while you follow along. As I read, you should listen to find out where these beavers live and why they live there. (The teacher reads aloud while students follow.)

Teacher: Please find the sentence that tells us where the beavers live. Who will read that sentence for us?

Nick: "Their home was a little island with a secret tunnel that went down into the water."

Teacher: Now find the sentence that tells us why they live on an island, and point to it. Who would like to read that for us?

Debbie: "The bears and the foxes and the great wild cats could not get them."

Teacher: Now let's all turn the page, and take a look at the picture. That is a picture of a beaver dam. What do you think it is made of?

Nick: It looks like sticks and stuff from the woods.

Teacher: Good. Dams made by beavers and by people serve important purposes. I would like for Laura to read the next page while we all follow along so we can find out why this dam is important.

Laura: "One spring evening, the father beaver woke up. Something was not right! The water in the lake was going down. He went into the tunnel and slipped down into the water. He swam across the lake to look at the dam."

Teacher: Who can tell us why the dam is important?

Chris: It holds the water to make a lake.

Teacher: Now let's turn to the next page. I think that you can whisper read this page by yourself. If you need my help, just point to the word that you are having difficulty with and I will help. As you read, think of a question that you could ask your partner about the page. You may begin.

(Students whisper read the next page.)

Teacher: Now I would like for you to turn to your partner, and ask each other one question about this page. Try to remember the answer without looking in the book. You have one minute. Go.

(The book is completed using alternatives demonstrated.)

Note: By alternating teacher read-alouds, individual student reading, whole-group whisper reading, or even partner reading, a variety of strategies can be practiced. When the teacher reads aloud, students have a good model for improving their own fluency while focusing more on comprehension. Students who read aloud individually are building fluency as well as practicing reading to an audience. When everyone is whisper reading at the same time, all the students are active readers with support given by the teacher. Reading with a partner offers students the opportunity to monitor the reading strategies used by another reader as they are put in a support role. Incorporating these reading alternatives helps students to remain focused as they interact with the text in a variety of ways.

See Figure 32 for a completed lesson plan for transitional readers.

FIGURE 32
Completed Reading Lesson Plan: Transitional Reader (Stage 4)

Group: D   Date: 2-18-03

	Comments
Rereading Level 1. Jessica in the Dark 16	Partner Read
Word Bank Completed 100 words	No specialized or hard vocabulary to preteach for new read.
Word Study Vowel Pattern Sort A patterns Vowel Pattern Concentration ✓ or Spell Check ✓ or Word Scramble ✓	Use header cards: cat make car
Writing (Sentence Dictation) Dad made a trap for the shark.	
New Read Level 1. The Busy Beavers 16	Alternate teacher read aloud, individual and whisper reading.

When to Move to the Next Stage

The move to the final stage, Independent Reader, could best be described as a leap. To be prepared to move ahead, students need to automatically recognize at least 100 words, completing the word bank. These students also should be able to write dictated sentences containing varied vowel patterns with accuracy and confidence. Independence—when students choose to read by themselves—is another indicator. Finally, the Reading Review should be completed to confirm that each student is reading at the appropriate instructional level.

Conclusion

Students' accomplishments in the Transitional Reader stage are extensive. The children have been transformed from being heavily dependent on the teacher to being confident readers. Developing strategies in decoding and comprehension have increased students' abilities to read independently. As these students transition to the Independent Reader stage, they will continue to focus on increasing skills in fluency, decoding, and comprehension.

CHAPTER 8

Stage 5: Independent Reader

Characteristics of Independent Readers

Independent readers begin to exhibit characteristics of mature readers—reading with speed, accuracy, and proper expression. They read independently from a variety of genres and for a variety of purposes. In this stage, readers use diverse strategies as they cope with challenges in more difficult text. Independent readers can skim text quickly to retrieve information as well as infer (read between the lines and draw conclusions) in their efforts to comprehend text. Without conscious attention, these students perform multiple reading tasks—such as word recognition and comprehension—at the same time.

Texts for Independent Readers

A variety of texts should be used with independent readers. Choose from a range of topics, formats, text types, and illustrative styles. Longer stories and chapter books with rich vocabulary and more fully developed plots should be used. Most illustrations at this level are used to establish mood rather than to support the story line. Fortunately, many of the companies publishing leveled books have been attentive to the need for text variation for independent readers, including many more nonfiction selections in their offerings. As reading maturity develops, a wider variety of reading material should be considered, including children's newspapers and magazines. Teachers should always be mindful of the supports and challenges presented in the text. The following are appropriate leveled books for independent readers:

Leveling System	Book Levels
Reading Recovery	17–20 +
DRA	18–28
Fountas and Pinnell	J–M

Instructional Strategies in the Independent Reader Lesson Plan

Easy Read/Reread (Optional)

The lesson plan model for independent readers has significant modifications to address the needs of these more accomplished readers. Rereading can now be replaced

FIGURE 33
Reading Lesson Plan: Independent Reader (Stage 5)

Group:____ Date:______________

Easy Read/Reread (optional) 1.______________________________	Comments
Word Study Word Pattern Sort____________________ Concentration______________________ or Spell Check________________________ or Word Scramble______________________	
Writing (Sentence Dictation) ______________________________	

New Read

Before

Hook ______________________________

____

Connection ______________________________

____

Hard Parts ______________________________

____

Purpose ______________________________

____

Predicting ______________________________

During

Question Points

Page ______________

Question______________________

Page ______________

Question______________________

Page ______________

Question______________________

After

Questions______________________

____

____

Summarize______________________

____

____

Responding______________________

____

____

or alternated with an easy read. An easy read provides an opportunity to continue work on oral reading fluency by reading material at the students' independent level. According to the National Reading Panel (National Institute of Child Health and Human Development, 2000), providing students with guided oral reading opportunities has significant impact on word recognition, fluency, and comprehension. As noted in the lesson plan, the easy read is optional. You might want to include the easy read on days when the new read is a short selection. Regardless, fluent readers should be given ample time to read independently during the school day.

- Choose a book (or parts of a book) slightly below the group's instructional level.
- Incorporate teacher modeling to develop fluency.
- Use this opportunity to have students practice as though they were reading to an audience.

Teacher: Last week, we read *Cat's Diary* (Eggleton, 1999), and I thought that it might be a good book for us to practice reading aloud. (Teacher distributes books.) Please look through the book, and find one page that you would like to read to the group. You have a couple minutes to make your choice and practice reading by yourself before we begin. While you do that, I'm going to choose my favorite part to read to you.

This example provides a quick and easy way to build reading fluency. The book *Cat's Diary* lends itself nicely to this activity because each page is set up as a daily journal entry. Short poems also are good sources for practicing reading fluency. Reading selected parts from a text saves time and keeps the lesson plan moving.

Word Study

Complete the word study with one-syllable vowel patterns (Level 1). After completing each vowel pattern for Level 1, complete Level 2 of the vowel patterns (note that *U* has no words for Level 2):

a	i	o	u	e
rain	right	told		meat
ball	by	moon		head
saw	find	boil		new
		low		
		loud		
		boy		

- Complete the vowel pattern sequence.
- Mix the various vowel patterns and do a sorting activity followed by Concentration, Spell Check (see Figure 34), or Word Scramble.

FIGURE 34
Students Participate in a Spell Check

- When the group completes the vowel pattern sequence, word study can be dropped or a more advanced word study including analogies, prefixes, suffixes, synonyms, or antonyms might be substituted.

Writing

Continue using the dictation sentences for Level 2 vowel patterns (see Appendix C, pp. 230–237) until the group completes the vowel pattern word study.

New Read

To adequately prepare students to read the text, it is critical that you preview the text prior to the reading group lesson. The strategies used before, during, and after the reading continue to expand and support the reader's literacy learning.

Before Reading

Hook: How will you excite the students about reading the book? This is called the "hook." The hook should be a part of planning the lesson and should not be thought of on the spur of the moment. Based on the nonfiction book *Bats* (Russell-Arnot, 1999), an appropriate hook could be the following: Have you ever seen a real bat? This story is about the only mammal that can fly. You won't believe what happens when these bats sleep! Make the hook so exciting that the students can't wait to get started.

Connection: To increase comprehension, it is important that students connect with the text. According to Keene and Zimmermann (1997) in their book *Mosaic of Thought: Teaching Comprehension in a Reader's Workshop*, there are three ways that students connect: text to self, text to text, and text to world. Using the book *Bats*, appropriate connecting questions might include the following:

- What do you know about bats? (text to self)
- Have you read another book about bats? (text to text)
- Have you seen bats on television? What were they doing? (text to world)

Each group member will probably connect with the title in an individual way.

Hard Parts: After previewing the book, pinpoint any part of the story or story structure that might be difficult for the group. The hard parts of *Bats* might include specialized vocabulary or story structure (see the following three vignettes for examples).

(The teacher has predetermined three vocabulary words that might be challenging to the group. These words (*nocturnal, migration, hibernation*) are written on index cards.

Teacher: I have three words that we need to look over before we start reading our story about bats. This is the first word. (Teacher holds up word *nocturnal.*) Does anyone recognize this word?

Jennifer: *Nocturnal.*

Teacher: Yes, the word is *nocturnal*. Do you know what it means if an animal is nocturnal?

Bill: Does it mean they lived a long time ago?

Teacher: No. An animal is nocturnal if it sleeps during the day and stays awake at night. Do you know another animal that is nocturnal?

Leslie: An owl.

(Using the same process, the teacher introduces and discusses the additional words.)

Purpose: Prior to the lesson, establish a purpose for reading the text. Depending on the material, the purpose will vary and may include reading for pleasure, reading to find information, or reading to find out what happens.

Predicting: As discussed previously, predicting is an important strategy in developing reading comprehension. Although predicting occurs before the reading, it also is important to check and revise predictions during the reading. The table of contents is an excellent source of predicting. For example, students could predict which animals eat bats after reading the chapter title, "Bats get eaten too!"

Sometimes it is difficult to make predictions in nonfiction books. In this book, the teacher could have the students do some predicting about two types of bats that they would be reading about in the book.

Teacher:	We will read about fruit bats and vampire bats in this book. Let's make some predictions about these two kinds of bats. Where do you think these bats might live?
Katie:	Bats live in caves.
Teacher:	Yes. What kind of food do you think these bats eat?
Jennifer:	They like to eat people's blood.
Teacher:	Do you think they like different kinds of food?
Katie:	I think they like to eat bugs.
Teacher:	As we read the book, we will see if our predictions are right or if we want to change them.

Teacher:	We have discussed the fact that this book is nonfiction; it is a true story about bats. Nonfiction books are usually written differently than fiction books. In this book, there is a table of contents. Everybody turn to the inside, and find the table of contents. How many chapters are in this book?
Megan:	Eleven.
Teacher:	In which chapter would we find information about what bats are afraid of?
Jennifer:	"Bats get eaten too!"
Teacher:	In which chapter would we find information on what bats like to eat?
Bill:	"Different bats eat different things."
Teacher:	How is a table of contents helpful to a reader?
Clint:	It can tell us what is in the book we will be reading.

Some discussion and preteaching of these more difficult concepts will help promote a more successful and enjoyable read.

During Reading

Question Points: While previewing the text, note three or four strategic points during the story for questioning. Include questions that call for students to predict, summarize, recall, and infer. These questions should be included on the lesson plan along with page numbers for stopping points.

Reading Alternatives: Continue to vary the strategies used for reading the text. Several options include

- Teacher read: Take a turn with the students to provide a model for fluency.
- Silent read: Have all the students read a couple of pages silently. Ask them to look for particular information as they read or after they read; have them return to the text to find answers to questions.

- Partner read: Pair the students and let them read alternate pages while you monitor. Continue to use stopping points to include questioning.
- Individual read: Call on individuals to read pages or paragraphs randomly so that students are unaware of when their turn is coming. Thus, students will stay focused on the material and you can provide focused reading feedback to the individual reader.

After Reading

There are several options to consider after students complete the reading selection.

Questions: Follow up with questions concerning predictions and inferences, or pose other questions requiring more critical thinking.

Summarize: Ask students to summarize the selection, revisiting important points. This summary also could be presented as a writing assignment.

Teacher: We learned a lot of interesting things about bats from this book. I want you to think about one interesting fact that you learned about bats. While you are thinking, I am going to draw a circle or a graphic organizer on the board and put the word *bats* in the middle to help organize our thoughts. Now, who would like to start us off? Leslie, what would you like to share?

Leslie: I learned that bats like to sleep during the day.

Teacher: You're right. Do you remember the new word for sleeping during the day?

Leslie: *Nocturnal.*

Teacher: Good memory. I'm going to put that word on our graphic organizer.

(Students add remaining facts as teacher adds them to the graphic organizer.)

Responding: Many selections lend themselves to an in-depth discussion on varied topics. Allow students the chance for verbal exchange, which will enhance their thinking processes as well as their abilities to communicate effectively. Responding can take the form of a piece of writing, drama, a piece of art, or even a musical composition (see Figure 35 for an example of a student's response to reading). Independent readers should be given a variety of options in responding to the text.

Teacher: When you go to your seats, I want you to write a five-sentence paragraph about bats in your reading response journal. I will leave our graphic organizer on the board if you want to use these facts, or you may choose to use your own.

Note: A reading response journal is useful at this stage as students respond in a variety of ways to the text.

FIGURE 35
A Student Responds to Reading With Writing and a Piece of Art

How you choose to follow up the reading may depend on time restraints or maturity of the students. Most important, provide a variety of activities that involve students in integrated reading and writing activities to increase literacy development.

See Figure 36 for a completed lesson plan for independent readers.

FIGURE 36
Completed Reading Lesson Plan: Independent Reader (Stage 5)

Group: E Date: 1-16-03

Easy Read/Reread (optional)

1. Cat's Diary (L) (A reread)

Comments

Each student will select page to read orally for fluency.

Word Study

Word Pattern Sort A patterns (level 2)

Concentration ✓

or

Spell Check

or

Word Scramble

header cards:

rain ball saw

Writing (Sentence Dictation)

New Read Bats

Before

Hook Today we are going to read about the only mammals that fly!

Connection We read another book earlier this year about bats.

Hard Parts Vocabulary: nocturnal, migration, hibernation

Purpose To find out facts about bats (use index to stimulate discussion—What do you want to know about bats?)

Predicting We will read about fruit bats and vampire bats. What do you predict they will eat?

During

Question Points

Page 3

Question What does nocturnal mean? Do you know another nocturnal animal?

Page 5

Question Name two ways that bats can move.

Page 7

Question Do you want to change your predictions about what fruit bats and vampire bats eat?

After

Questions How many continents do bats live on? How are bats harmful?

Summarize Use graphic organizer—Students contribute one fact about bats.

Responding (Completed individually) Write a short paragraph on bats using the graphic organizer.

Conclusion

Although the Independent Reader stage is the last stage discussed in the Small-Group Differentiated Reading Model, this does not mean that independent readers are capable of reading any text presented to them. Fluency for a second-grade reader is very different from fluency for a fifth-grade reader. However, if we, as educators, are successful in bringing students to this basic independent level of literacy learning, the doors will open to a world of rich literary experiences.

CONCLUSION

The question of how to teach beginning readers may be the most politically charged topic in education. Over the past decade, U.S. society has become more focused on successful reading instruction. This concern was evidenced most recently in President Bush's No Child Left Behind legislation. Accountability lies in the forefront of this legislation, but without solid, research-based instruction in place, we certainly will continue to miss the mark.

Every child deserves the opportunity to receive quality reading instruction—reading instruction that transforms him or her into a competent reader. Reading is the key that unlocks future educational opportunities for all students. Although all students may not elect to attend a college or university, most will join the workforce and become parents of children who will need to be read to and nurtured in a literate environment.

Although some children learn to read prior to explicit reading instruction, many do not. For these children, there is not a classroom moment to waste. If we are to accomplish the lofty goal of making every child a successful reader, educators must be diligent in designing and implementing comprehensive reading programs. Small-group differentiated reading instruction can be used to effectively address the potential problems and serve the important purpose of reducing reading failure. Grouping students of similar reading abilities helps teachers plan instruction that best matches students' needs. This reading instruction must be consistent and provide students with opportunities to engage in contextual reading as well as systematic word study that is carefully paced to maximize learning opportunities. When children have a strong literacy foundation, the educational opportunities become endless.

This book presents step-by-step lesson plans reflecting the developmental stages of the reading process that will assist teachers in planning for meaningful instruction in primary-grade classrooms. Although this book contains many familiar, research-based strategies, it is not in these individual strategies alone that we find the strength of the Small-Group Differentiated Reading Model. The power is found in the way in which these strategies are pieced together and structured to support one another.

I believe that teachers are in need of useful, research-based models that can be easily adapted for classroom implementation. My observations have led me to believe that most teachers are overwhelmed by the demands of students, parents, administrators, and even legislators, leaving little time for reading and studying the current research. Expecting teachers to develop quality, research-based instructional models prior to actually teaching is like asking actors to perform Shakespeare but to write the play first.

There is no reading manual that can accurately tell a teacher everything to say or do. In my attempt to simplify the very complex reading process, I acknowledge and emphasize the unique needs of each student. I do, however, feel that the approach presented in this book might help lay the foundation on which teachers can begin to build effective reading programs for all students.

I am first and foremost a teacher. Like most teachers, I am seeking solutions to teach all children how to read. Given appropriate instruction, I am confident that we can significantly increase the number of students reading at or above grade level by the end of third grade. If this book helps only one teacher to teach one child to read, it was well worth the effort.

Early Reading Screening Instrument Materials

Note: Materials in bold type are included in this appendix and may be duplicated for classroom use.

EARLY READING SCREENING INSTRUMENT
ABBREVIATED TEACHER DIRECTIONS

1.1 ALPHABET

Recognition

Procedure: Point to letters; student names them.

Scoring:

Error	Marking	Example
doesn't know	circle	(k)
wrong letter	write above	J G
self-correction	check (✓)	m✓ n

All reversals count as errors. Self-corrections count as correct answers. Enter totals for upper- and lowercase alphabet recognition in the Alphabet score box at the top of the Individual Score Sheet (see p. 128).

Production

Procedure: Call out letter; student writes upper- **or** lowercase letter.

Scoring: Mark as student writes.
Write errors above letter on score sheet.
Circle if no attempt is made.

Left-right reversal counts correct *(b-d).*
Up-down reversal counts as **error** *(p-d).*
Self-corrections count as correct answers.
Enter totals for upper- and lowercase alphabet recognition in the Alphabet score box at the top of the Individual Score Sheet (see p. 128).

1.2 CONCEPT OF WORD (The Katie Book)

Procedure: Ask student what the picture shows.

1. Finger-point read page 1.
2. Student finger-point reads page 1.
3. Point to underlined words in numerical order, and have student identify the words.
4. Proceed to pages 2 and 3, following above steps on each page.

Scoring: Pointing: ✓ or 0 (must read and point correctly to each word: self-corrections count as correct answers.)

Word: ✓ or 0 or write in incorrect word.

Scores on this section are combined with scores on *My Home* task.

See section 2.1, Scoring.

1.3 WORD RECOGNITION (Basal Words)

Procedure: Hold index card below each word and have student read the word. (Note: Stop if no response is given to first four words.)

Scoring: ✓ or 0 or write in incorrect word.

Count ✓'s.

Enter total (number of checks) in the Word Recognition box at the top of the Individual Score Sheet (see p. 128).

2.1 CONCEPT OF WORD (*My Home*)

Procedure: Read the title to introduce the book. Have student name the animal pictures on pages 2–5. As pages 6–7 are turned to, cover page 7 with hand. Ask student to predict what the dog and rabbit will do, then reveal page 7. Return to page 2 to begin reading.

1. Finger-point read page 2.
2. Student attempts to finger point and read page 2.
3. Point to word underlined on score sheet for page 2. Student attempts to read it. (Teacher records responses.)
4. Follow same procedures on page 3.

(Note: On pages 4, 5, and 7, student reads on his or her own. On page 4 only, you may help if needed by placing student's finger on the word *my* and saying "my." *You* may read pages 6 and 8 to child.)

Scoring: Same as section **1.2**

Count ✓'s for pointing in sections **1.2** and **2.1**. Enter total for pointing in the Concept of Word score box at the top of the Individual Score Sheet (see p. 128).

Count ✓'s for identifying words in sections **1.2** and **2.1**. Enter total for identifying words in the Concept of Word score box at the top of the Individual Score Sheet (see p. 128).

2.2 PHONEME AWARENESS (Spelling)

Procedure: Model spelling of sample words (*mat, lip*) by asking student to think about what letter comes first, second, and so on. (Write the words.)

1. Give student a pencil, and begin to dictate the 12 words.
2. Student attempts to spell each word on his or her own.
3. You may only help once on words #1 or #2. No help is given on remaining words. Observe spelling, and ask student to identify any letters that are unreadable.

(Note: If the student fails to provide the initial consonant on the sample words and each of the two test words, stop the spelling test.)

Scoring: Copy words as student writes.

See Scoring Guide. Enter the total number of points in the Phoneme Awareness score box at the top of the Individual Score Sheet (see p. 130).

2.3 WORD RECOGNITION (Decodable Words)

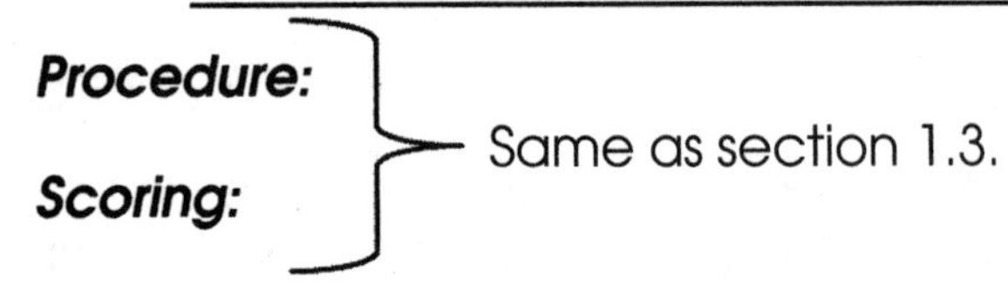

Procedure:

Scoring:

Same as section 1.3.

CALCULATING TOTALS	
ALPHABET KNOWLEDGE $\frac{a+b+c}{78}$ x 10 = TOTAL	**PHONEME AWARENESS** $\frac{f}{42}$ x 10 = TOTAL
CONCEPT OF WORD $\frac{d+e}{16}$ x 10 = TOTAL	**WORD RECOGNITION** $\frac{g+h}{20}$ x 10 = TOTAL
Round to nearest 10th; .05's round up. Add four TOTALS to calculate GRAND TOTAL.	

SCORING GUIDE FOR PHONEME AWARENESS (Spelling)

One point is awarded for each phoneme represented by an appropriate letter. Examiners will need to interpret spellings if no example below matches child's attempt. Phonemes represented out of order are not awarded points. Note maximum points per word varies from 3 to 4.

Spelling Word	1 point	2 points	3 points	4 points
1. back	B, BN	BC, BK, BA, BAE, BIG, BOC	BAC, BAK, BAKE, BACK	
2. feet	F, FA	FT, FE, FIT	FET, FEAT, FETE, FEET	
3. step	S, C, SOT	ST, CP, SA, SE	STP, SAP, CAP, CAP, STIP	STAP, SDAP, STEP
4. junk	J, G	JK, GC, JO, GU	JOK, GOK, GNK, JIJK	JONC, GUNK
5. picking	P, PO	PK, PC, PE, PN	PEC, PEK, PIK, PEN, PKN	PECN, PICEN, PEKN, PICKING
6. mail	M, MI	ML, MA, MAO, ME	MAL, MAOL, MALE, MEL, MAIL	
7. side	5, C, ST	SE, CD, SACC, SED	SID, CID, SAD, SOD, SIDE	
8. chin	G, J, H	GN, IN, HN, GAN	GEN, HIN, CHEN, CHIN	
9. dress	D, J, G	JS, GD, DOS	JAS, DES, IRS, DRS, DESS, GAS	DRAS, JRES, DRES, DRESS
10. peeked	P	PT, PE, PK, KIT	PET, PCT, PEK, PIKT, PEET	PECT, PEKED, PEEKT, PEEKED
11. lamp	L	LP, LA, LOP, LM	LAP, LAPE, LAM, LMP	LAMPE, LAMP
12. road	R, W, RT	RD, RO	ROD, ROED, RODE, ROAD	

Reprinted from Morris, D. (1998). Assessing printed word knowledge in beginning readers: The Early Reading Screening Instrument (ERSI). *Illinois Reading Council Journal, 26*(2), pp. 30–40.

EARLY READING SCREENING INSTRUMENT CLASS TALLY SHEET

SCHOOL ______________________ TEACHER ______________________ DATE ______________

SCREENING SCORES - ERSI

	ALPHABET KNOWLEDGE				CONCEPT OF WORD			PHONEME AWARENESS		WORD RECOGNITION				
NAME	Upper 26	Lower 26	Prod. 26	TOTAL	Point 8	Word 8	TOTAL	Count 42	TOTAL	Basal 10	Dec. 10	TOTAL	GRAND TOTAL	Teacher Comments

EARLY READING SCREENING INSTRUMENT FOLDER CUT-OUTS

EARLY READING SCREENING INSTRUMENT
TESTING MATERIALS

FOLDER INCLUDES

1.1 Alphabet Recognition and Production

1.3 Word Recognition (Basal Words)

2.3 Word Recognition (Decodable Words)

(For convenience, other ERSI materials also may be stored in this folder.)

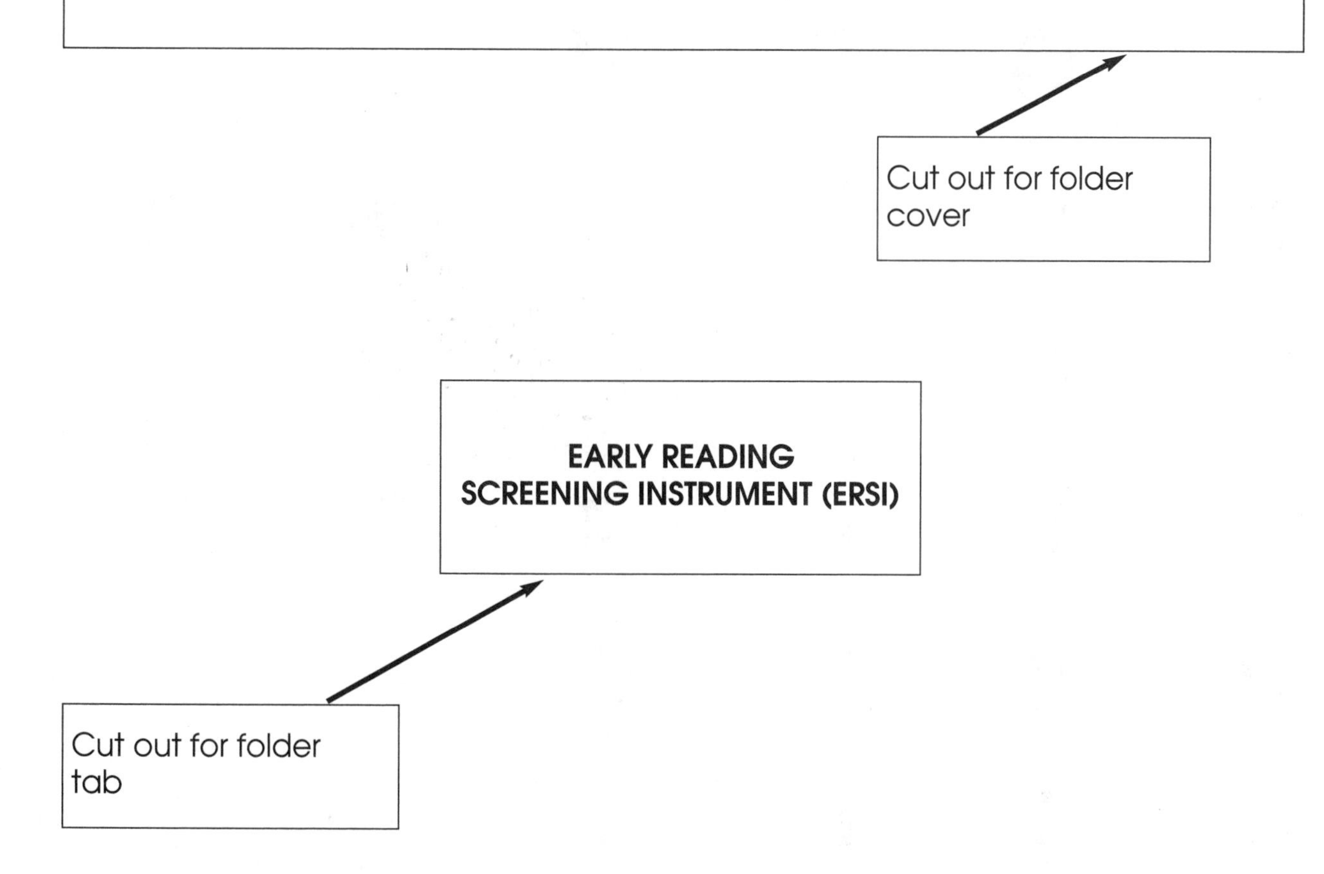

1.1 ALPHABET RECOGNITION AND PRODUCTION

A	F	K	P	W	Z
B	H	O	J	U	
C	Y	L	Q	M	
D	N	S	X	I	
E	G	R	V	T	

a	f	k	p	w	z
b	h	o	j	u	
c	y	l	q	m	
d	n	s	x	i	
e	g	r	v	t	

Adapted from Morris, D. (1998). Assessing printed word knowledge in beginning readers: The Early Reading Screening Instrument (ERSI). *Illinois Reading Council Journal, 26*(2), 30–40.

1.2 CONCEPT OF WORD (The Katie Book)

Reprinted from Morris, D. (1998). Assessing printed word knowledge in beginning readers: The Early Reading Screening Instrument (ERSI). *Illinois Reading Council Journal, 26*(2), 30–40.

1.3 WORD RECOGNITION (Basal Words)

1. is
2. come
3. good
4. here
5. like
6. and
7. mother
8. make
9. work
10. day

2.1 CONCEPT OF WORD (*My Home*)

(*continued*)

My Home by June Melser (1998) reprinted with permission from Wright Group/McGraw-Hill. Available from Wright Group, 19201 120th Avenue N.E., Bothell, WA 98011-9512, phone 800-648-2970.

2.1 CONCEPT OF WORD (*My Home* continued)

My Home by June Melser (1998) reprinted with permission from Wright Group/McGraw-Hill. Available from Wright Group, 19201 120th Avenue N.E., Bothell, WA 98011-9512, phone 800-648-2970.

2.3 WORD RECOGNITION (Decodable Words)

1. cap
2. net
3. win
4. bug
5. fat
6. mop
7. led
8. dig
9. job
10. mud

EARLY READING SCREENING INSTRUMENT
INDIVIDUAL SCORE SHEET

School ______________________ Student Name ______________________

Examiner ______________________ Classroom Teacher ______________________

ALPHABET KNOWLEDGE				CONCEPT OF WORD			PHONEME AWARENESS		WORD RECOGNITION			GRAND TOTAL
Upper 26	Lower 26	Prod. 26	TOTAL	Point 8	Word 8	TOTAL	Count 42	TOTAL	Basal 10	Decodable 10	TOTAL	
___ (a)	___ (b)	___ (c)	(___)	___ (d)	___ (e)	(___)	___ (f)	(___)	___ (g)	___ (h)	(___)	

1.1 ALPHABET

RECOGNITION:

A F K P W Z B H O J U C Y L Q M

D N S X L E G R V T

CORRECT ___ /26 (a)

a f k p w z b h o j u c y l q m

d n s x l e g r v t

CORRECT ___ /26 (b)

PRODUCTION:

A F K P W Z B H O J U C Y L Q M

D N S X L E G R V T

CORRECT ___ /26 (c)

(continued)

EARLY READING SCREENING INSTRUMENT
INDIVIDUAL SCORE SHEET (continued)

1.2 CONCEPT OF WORD (The Katie Book)

		Point		Words
1. Katie is walking[1] in the rain[2].	________	1 ________		2 ________
2. She[1] sees a big[2] dog.	________	1 ________		2 ________
3. The dog[2] shakes water[1] on Katie.	________	1 ________		2 ________

Scores are combined with section 2.1. When test is completed, count ✓s for pointing & words. Record in Concept of Word box in Individual Score Sheet.

1.3 WORD RECOGNITION (Basal Words)

1. is ________	4. here ________	7. mother ________	10. day ________
2. come ________	5. like ________	8. make ________	
3. good ________	6. and ________	9. work ________	

CORRECT
_____ /10
(g)

2.1 CONCEPT OF WORD (*My Home*)

Page		Point	Word
(2)	"My home is here." said the bird.	________	________
(3)	"My home is here." said the frog.	________	________
(4)	"My home is here," said the pig.	________	
(5)	"My home is here," said the dog.	________	
(7)	"My home is here," said the rabbit.	________	

Note: Count ✓'s for pointing and words from sections 1.2 and 2.1 and record totals below.
CORRECT (point) _____/8
(d)
My Home
CORRECT (word)_____/8
(e)

(continued)

Reprinted from Morris, D. (1998). Assessing printed word knowledge in beginning readers: The Early Reading Screening Instrument (ERSI). *Illinois Reading Council Journal, 26*(2), 30–40.

EARLY READING SCREENING INSTRUMENT
INDIVIDUAL SCORE SHEET (continued)

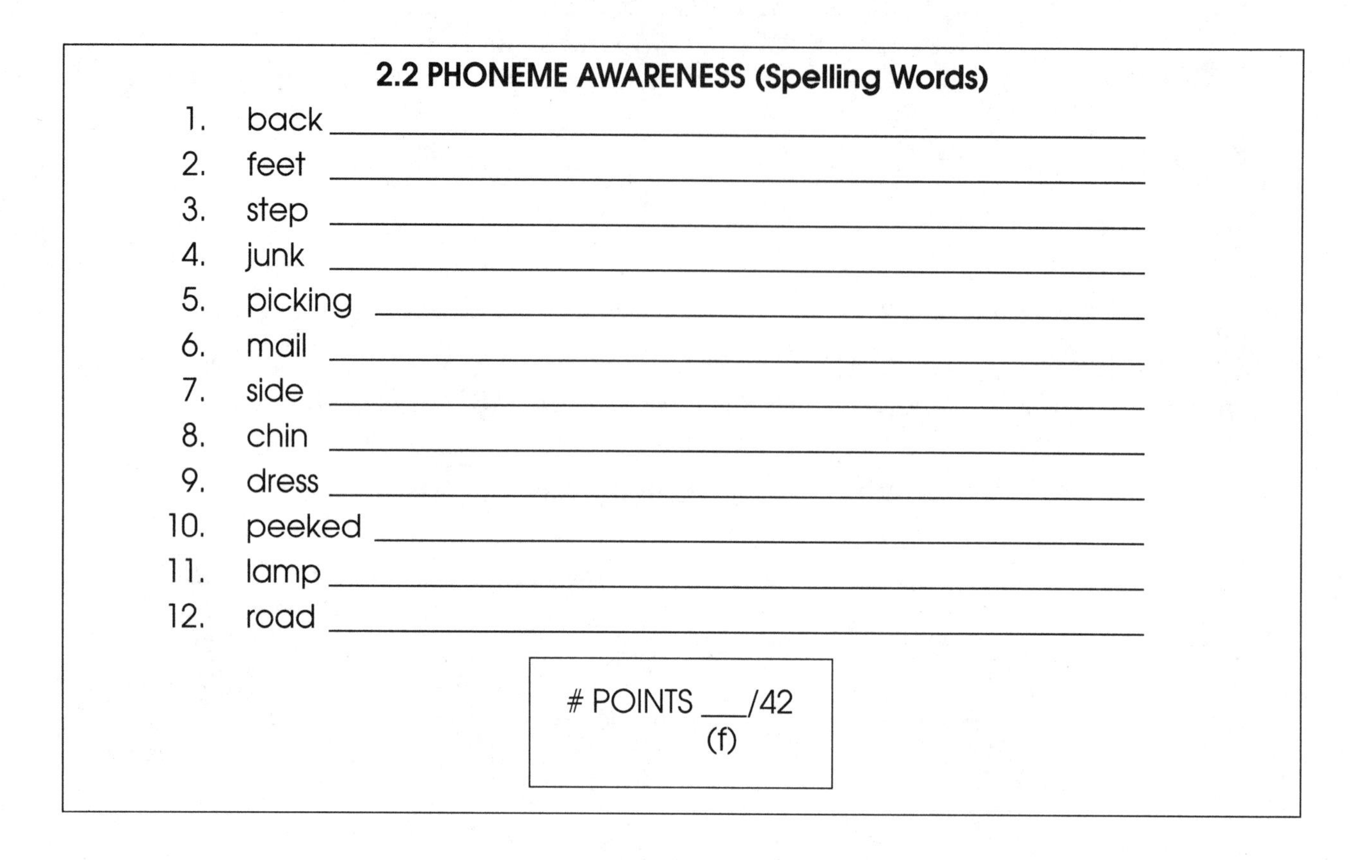

2.2 PHONEME AWARENESS (Spelling Words)

1. back ____________________
2. feet ____________________
3. step ____________________
4. junk ____________________
5. picking ____________________
6. mail ____________________
7. side ____________________
8. chin ____________________
9. dress ____________________
10. peeked ____________________
11. lamp ____________________
12. road ____________________

POINTS ___/42
(f)

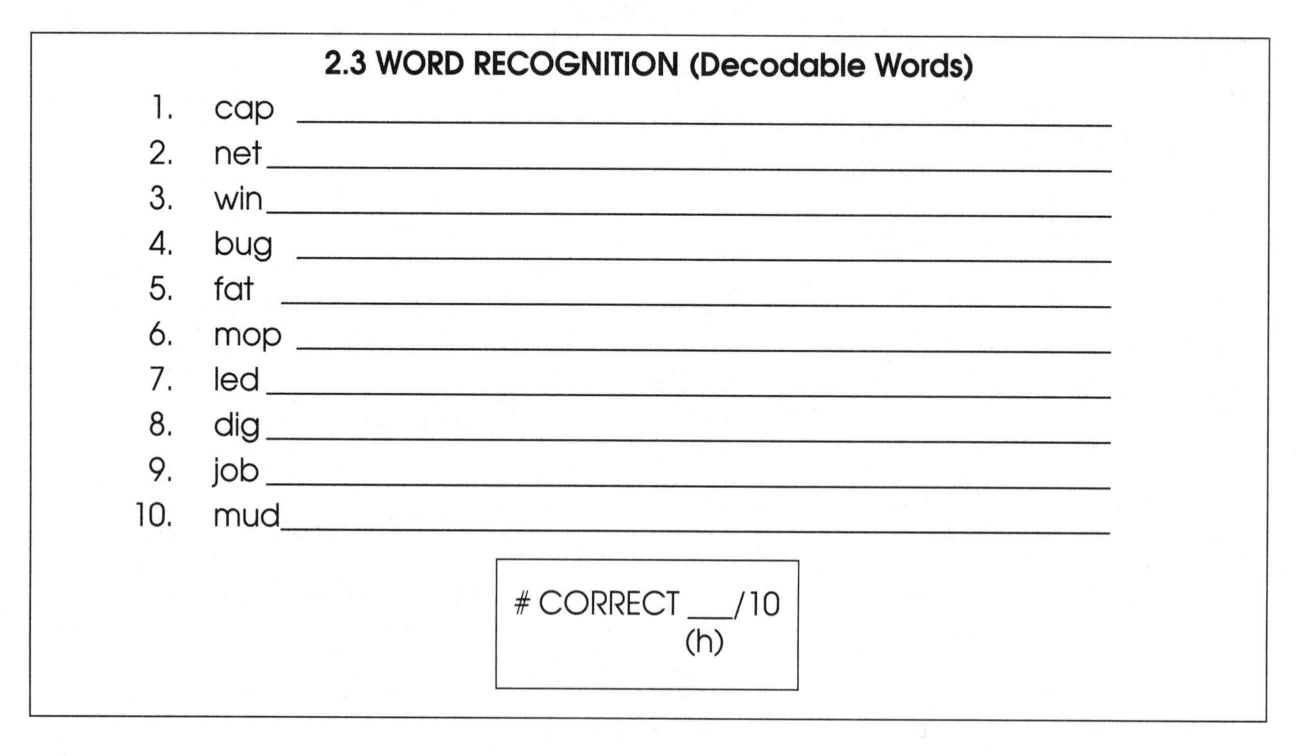

2.3 WORD RECOGNITION (Decodable Words)

1. cap ____________________
2. net ____________________
3. win ____________________
4. bug ____________________
5. fat ____________________
6. mop ____________________
7. led ____________________
8. dig ____________________
9. job ____________________
10. mud ____________________

CORRECT ___/10
(h)

ALPHABET PRODUCTION SHEET

Name ______________________________

★ ______________________________

____

____

____

SPELLING ANSWER SHEET

1. ______________ 7. ______________

2. ______________ 8. ______________

3. ______________ 9. ______________

4. ______________ 10. ______________

5. ______________ 11. ______________

6. ______________ 12. ______________

APPENDIX B

Word Study Materials

Note: Materials in this appendix may be duplicated for classroom use.

LETTER CARDS

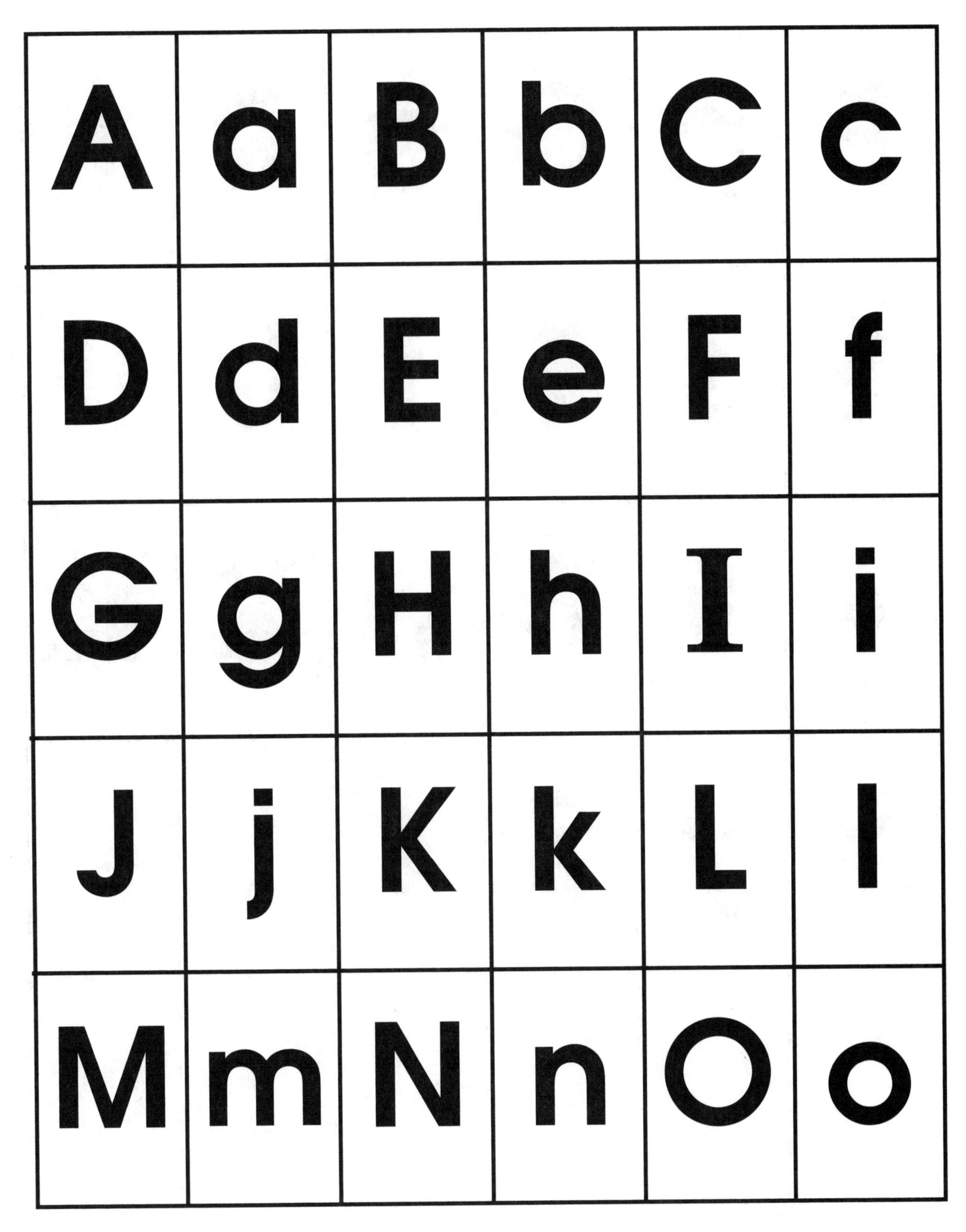

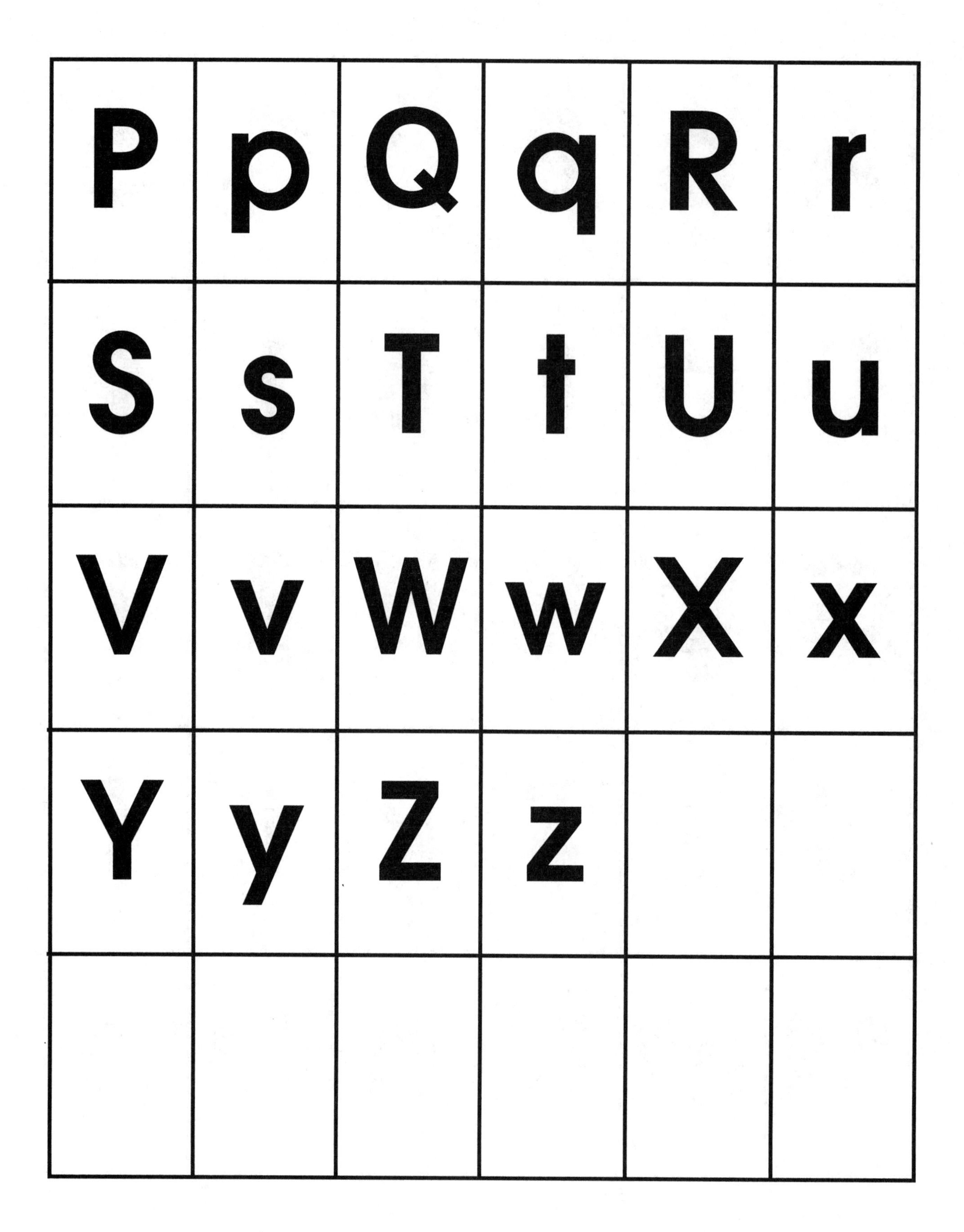
P p Q q R r
S s T t U u
V v W w X x
Y y Z z

PICTURE CARDS

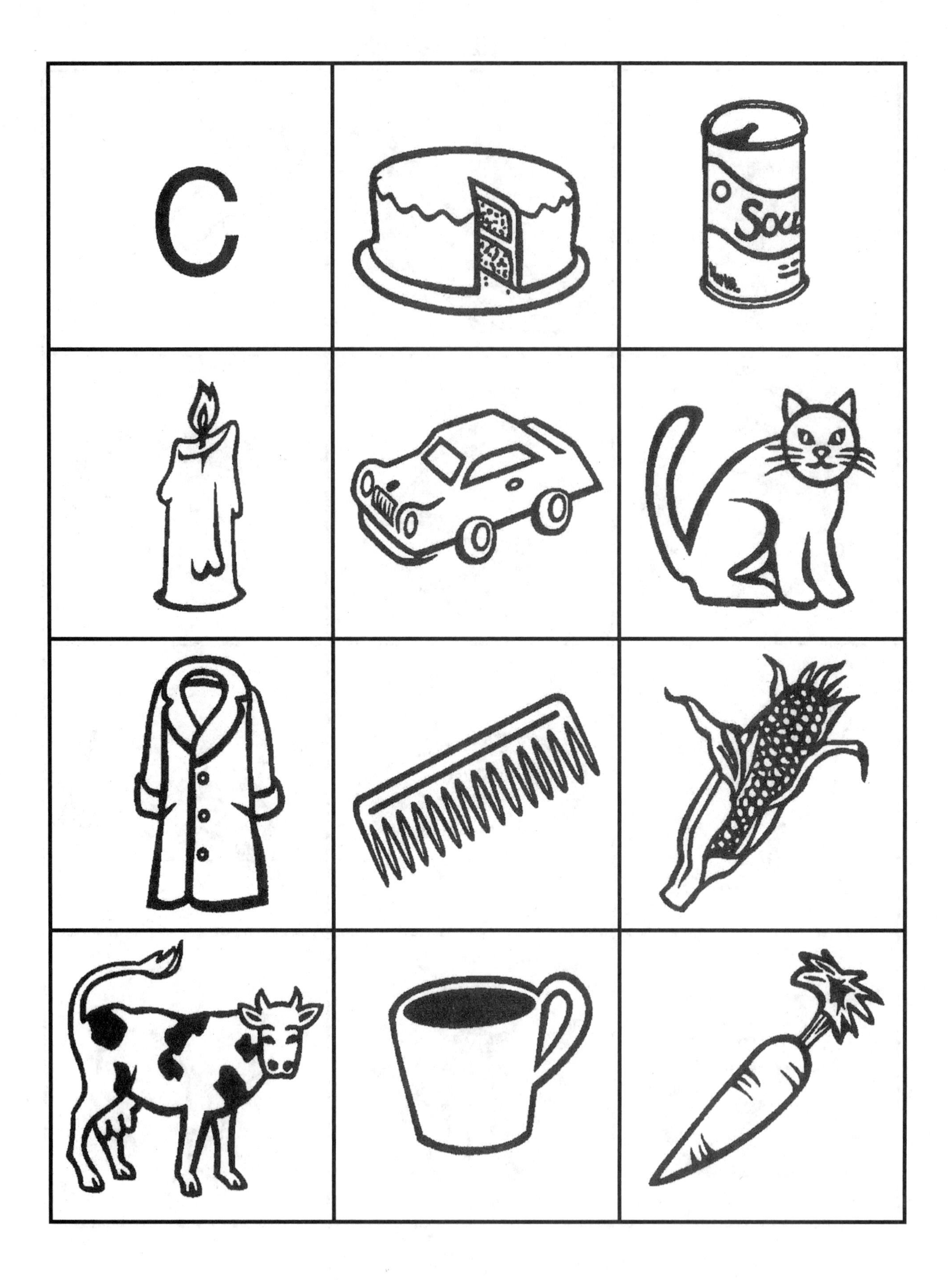
C
Sou

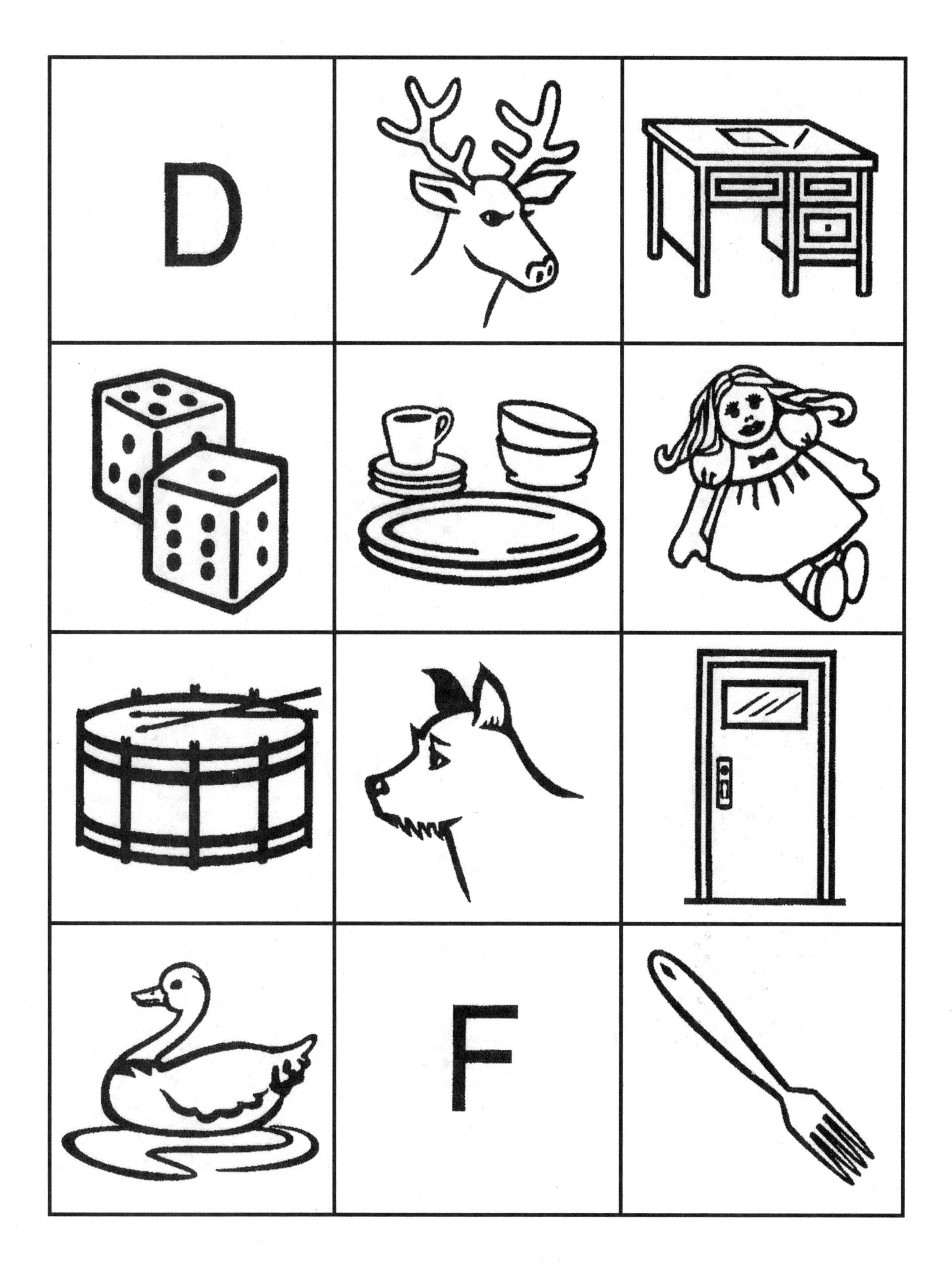
D
F

4
5
G
PREMIUM

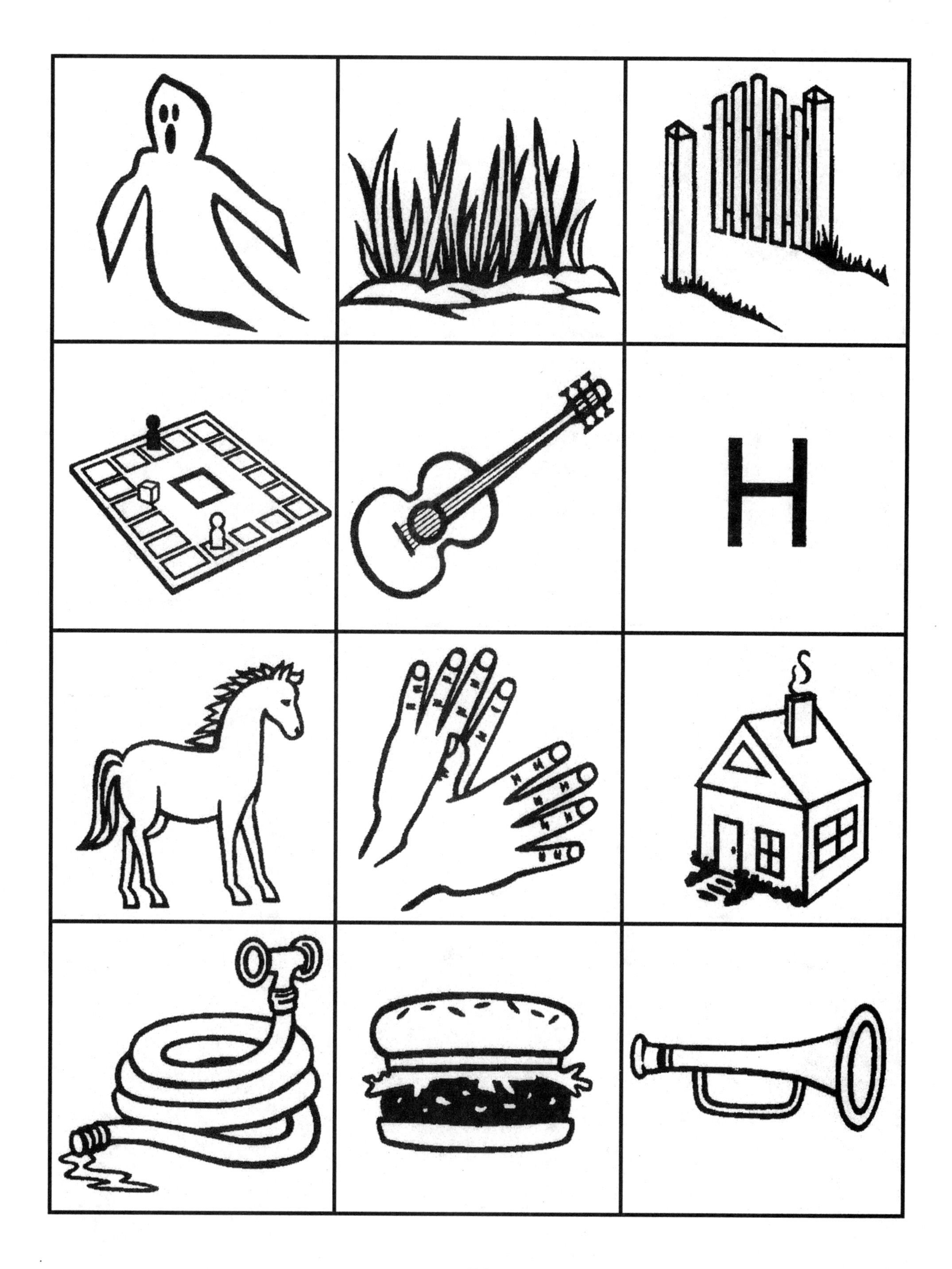
H

J

K
L

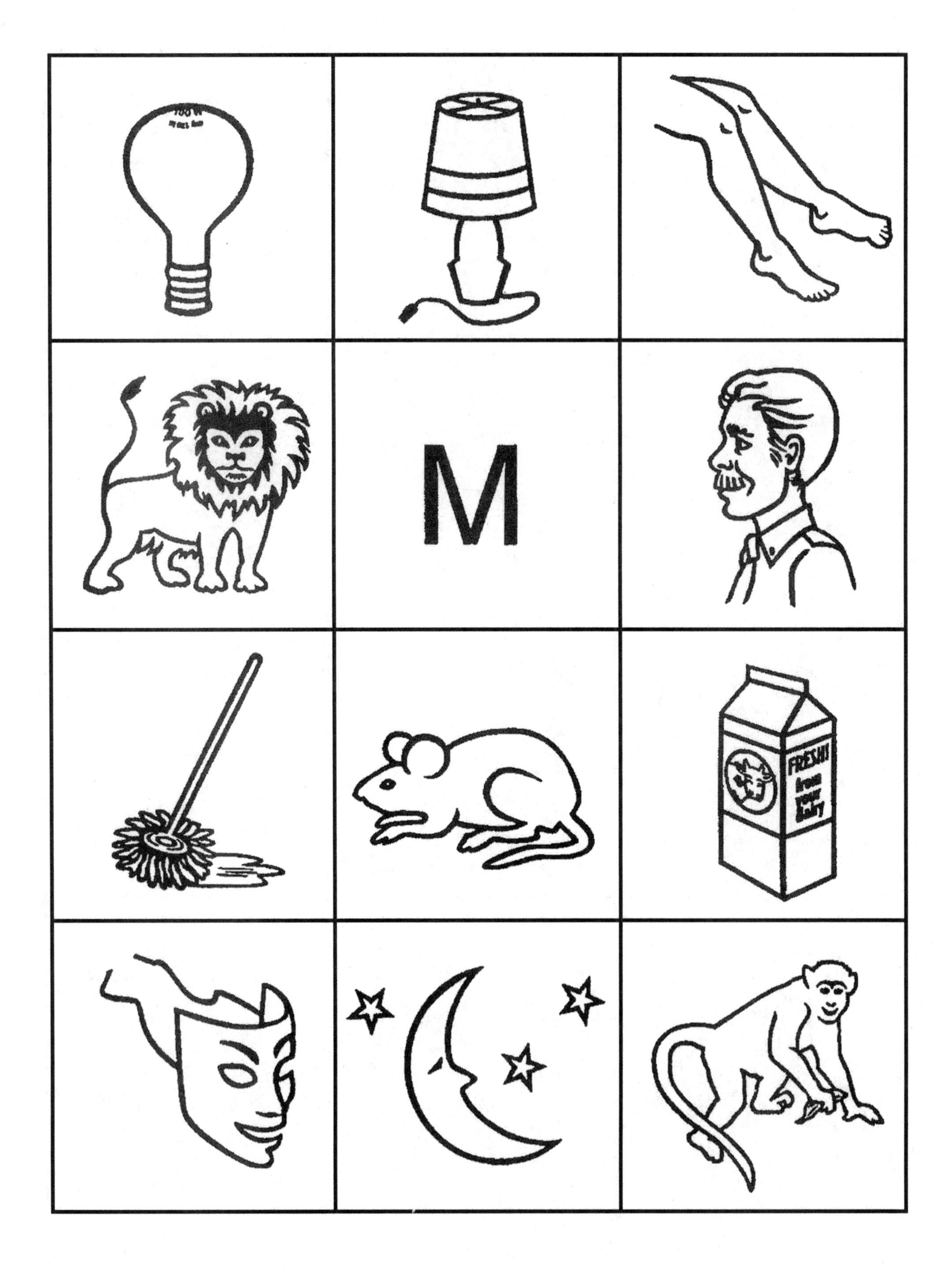
M
FRESH!
from
your
dairy

UNITED
STATES
N
N
9

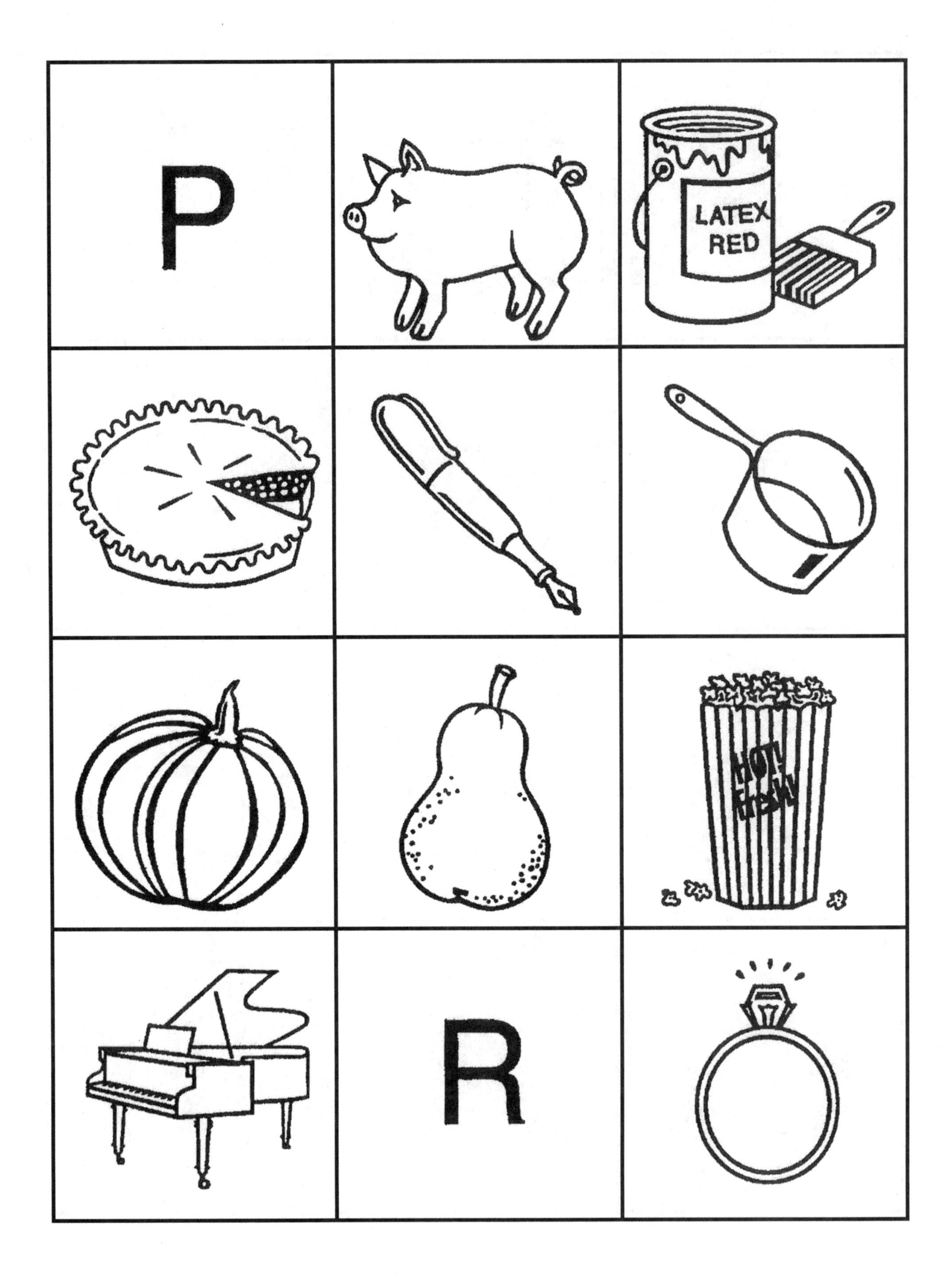
P
LATEX
RED
HOT!
Fresh!
R

S

6
T
2

10
V
THE THREE BEARS
I LOVE YOU

W
Y

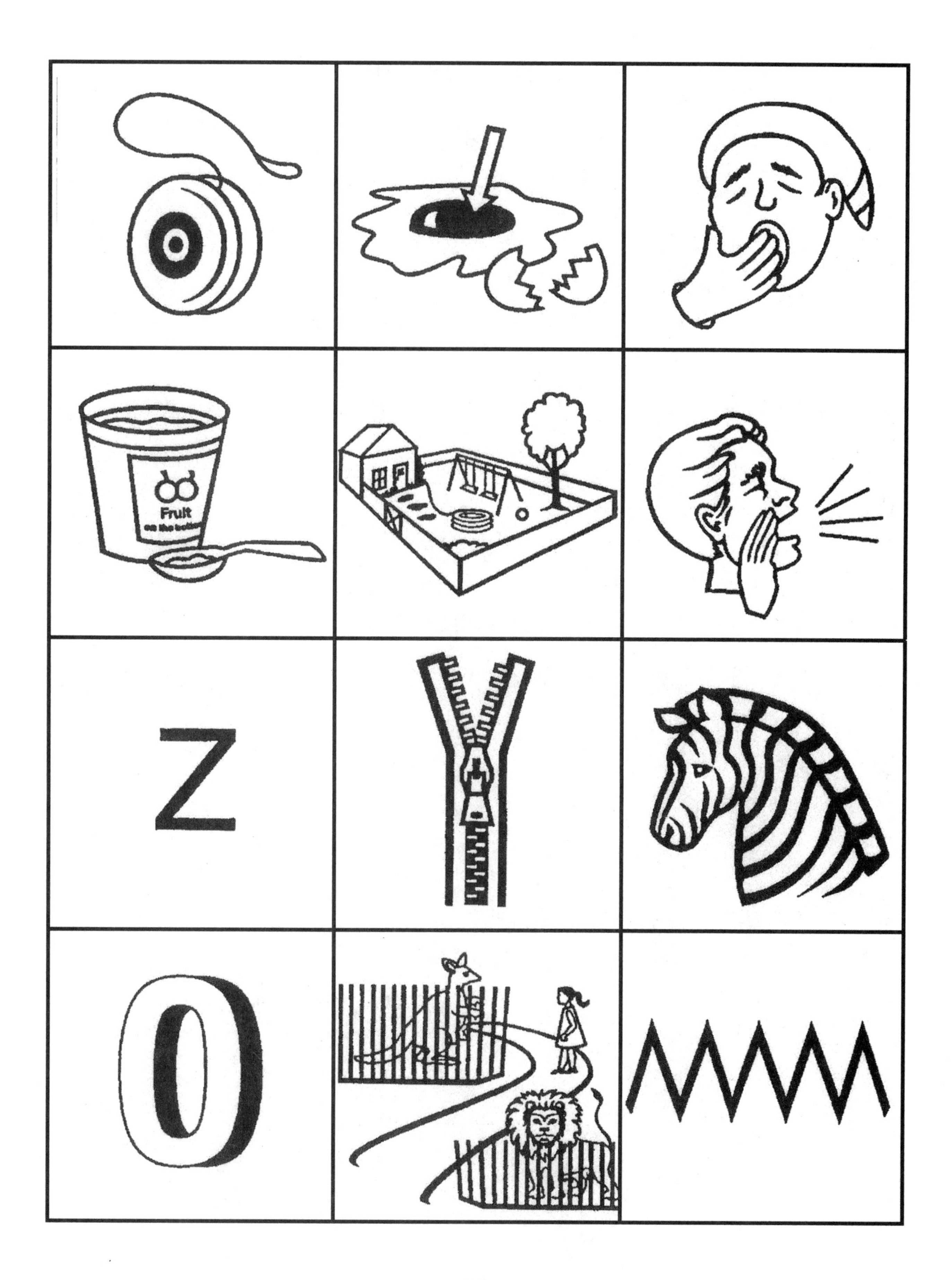
Fruit
Z
O

WORD STUDY LISTS

Word Families

A Families

cat	**man**	**cap**	**back**
mat	can	nap	tack
sat	ran	lap	rack
pat	van	tap	sack
bat	fan	map	pack
rat	pan	sap	black
hat	tan	clap	track
flat	plan	snap	snack

I Families

hit	**big**	**win**	**sick**
sit	wig	tin	kick
fit	dig	pin	lick
pit	pig	kin	pick
kit	fig	fin	tick
bit	jig	chin	trick
spit	twig	thin	brick
knit		spin	stick
		skin	thick

O Families

hot	**top**	**Bob**	**sock**
pot	pop	lob	rock
lot	cop	cob	lock
dot	hop	job	dock
not	mop	mob	block
got	stop	rob	clock
spot	drop		knock
shot	chop		

U Families

cut	**bug**	**run**	**duck**
but	dug	bun	buck
hut	hug	fun	luck
nut	mug	gun	suck
shut	rug	run	tuck
	tug	sun	stuck
	slug	spun	truck
	plug		cluck

E Families

pet	**red**	**hen**	**tell**
bet	bed	den	bell
get	fed	men	fell
jet	led	pen	sell
let	shed	ten	well
met	sled	then	shell
net		when	
set			
wet			

Short-Vowel Words

bad	**pig**	**mom**	**bus**	**pet**
hat	win	hot	cup	bed
ran	hit	job	nut	let
map	lip	top	fun	red
mad	kid	hop	cut	web
back	his	fox	bug	tell
had	sick	doll	but	less
has	pick	chop	shut	then
that	ship	shop	truck	bell
glad	swim	drop	must	shell

<u>A</u> Vowel Patterns

Level 1

cat	**make**	**car**	**day**
ran	lake	park	say
dad	race	hard	may
hat	tape	barn	way
cab	page	jar	pay
flat	same	card	clay
clap	name	far	stay
back	take	part	play
trap	gave	farm	tray
that	shake	shark	stray

<u>A</u> Vowel Patterns

Level 2

rain	**ball**	**saw**
mail	fall	law
wait	hall	paw
pain	mall	raw
tail	tall	jaw
sail	wall	draw
paid	call	straw
gain	small	drawn
paint		
chain		

<u>I</u> Vowel Patterns

Level 1

hid	**ride**	**girl**
lip	nice	dirt
win	bike	bird
big	five	sir
hit	mile	first
pin	side	shirt
fit	drive	third
kick	mine	thirst
swim	dime	firm
chin	wise	birth

<u>I</u> Patterns

Level 2

right	**by**	**find**
night	my	mind
light	fly	kind
might	dry	blind
high	cry	mild
tight	sky	child
flight	shy	wild
bright	spy	grind
fight	try	climb

O Vowel Patterns

Level 1

mom	**rope**	**go**	**for**	**boat**	**look**	**cow**
dot	note	no	cord	coat	book	how
job	hole	so	fork	moat	good	town
pot	nose		born	soap	foot	plow
top	coke		fort	load	stood	brown
drop	hope		port	coal	hook	crown
lock	bone		torn	soak	brook	tower
stop	code		sport	toast	wood	owl
bomb	woke			float		
shock	spoke			coach		

O Vowel Patterns

Level 2

told	**moon**	**boil**	**low**	**loud**	**boy**
cold	roof	coin	tow	south	toy
colt	pool	soil	snow	sound	joy
gold	boot	point	grow	mouth	soy
fold	tool	noise	show	shout	Roy
sold	shoot	spoil	flow	count	
hold	tooth	voice	blow		
mold	broom				

U Vowel Patterns

Levels 1–2

mud	**cute**	**hurt**	**blue**
cup	use	curl	true
bus	tune	fur	glue
fun	huge	burn	Sue
rug	June	turn	clue
sun	fuse	nurse	
bug	mule	curve	
club		purse	

E Vowel Patterns

Level 1

red	**feet**	**her**	**he**
ten	deep	germ	we
beg	meet	herd	she
get	feel	clerk	me
bell	free	nerve	be
less	green	serve	
next	seed		
left	need		
pet	queen		
step	jeep		

E Vowel Patterns

Level 2

meat	**head**	**new**
team	lead	grew
lead	bread	few
mean	dead	chew
peak	deaf	flew
clean	breath	blew
beat	spread	stew
dream	sweat	brew
beach		dew
leaf		drew

WORD FAMILY CARDS

Short A Family

cat*	man*	cap*
mat	can	nap
sat	ran	lap
pat	van	tap
bat	fan	map

Short <u>A</u> Family

rat	pan	sap
hat	tan	clap
flat	plan	snap

Short A Family

back*	black	
tack	track	
rack	snack	
sack		
pack		

Short I Family

hit*	big*	win*
sit	wig	tin
fit	dig	pin
pit	pig	kin
kit	fig	fin

Short I Family

bit	jig	chin
knit	twig	thin
		spin
		skin

Short I Family

sick*	trick	
kick	brick	
lick	stick	
pick	thick	
tick		

Short O Family

hot*	top*	Bob*
pot	pop	lob
lot	cop	cob
dot	hop	job
not	mop	mob

Short O Family

got	stop	rob
spot	drop	
shot	chop	

Short O Family

sock*	clock	
rock	knock	
lock		
dock		
block		

Short U Family

cut*	bug*	run*
but	dug	bun
hut	hug	fun
nut	mug	gun
shut	rug	

Short U Family

	tug	sun
	slug	spun
	plug	

Short U Family

duck*	truck	
buck	stuck	
luck		
suck		
tuck		

Short E Family

pet*	red*	hen*
bet	bed	den
get	fed	men
jet	led	pen
let	shed	ten

Short E Family

met	sled	then
net		when
set		
wet		

Short E Family

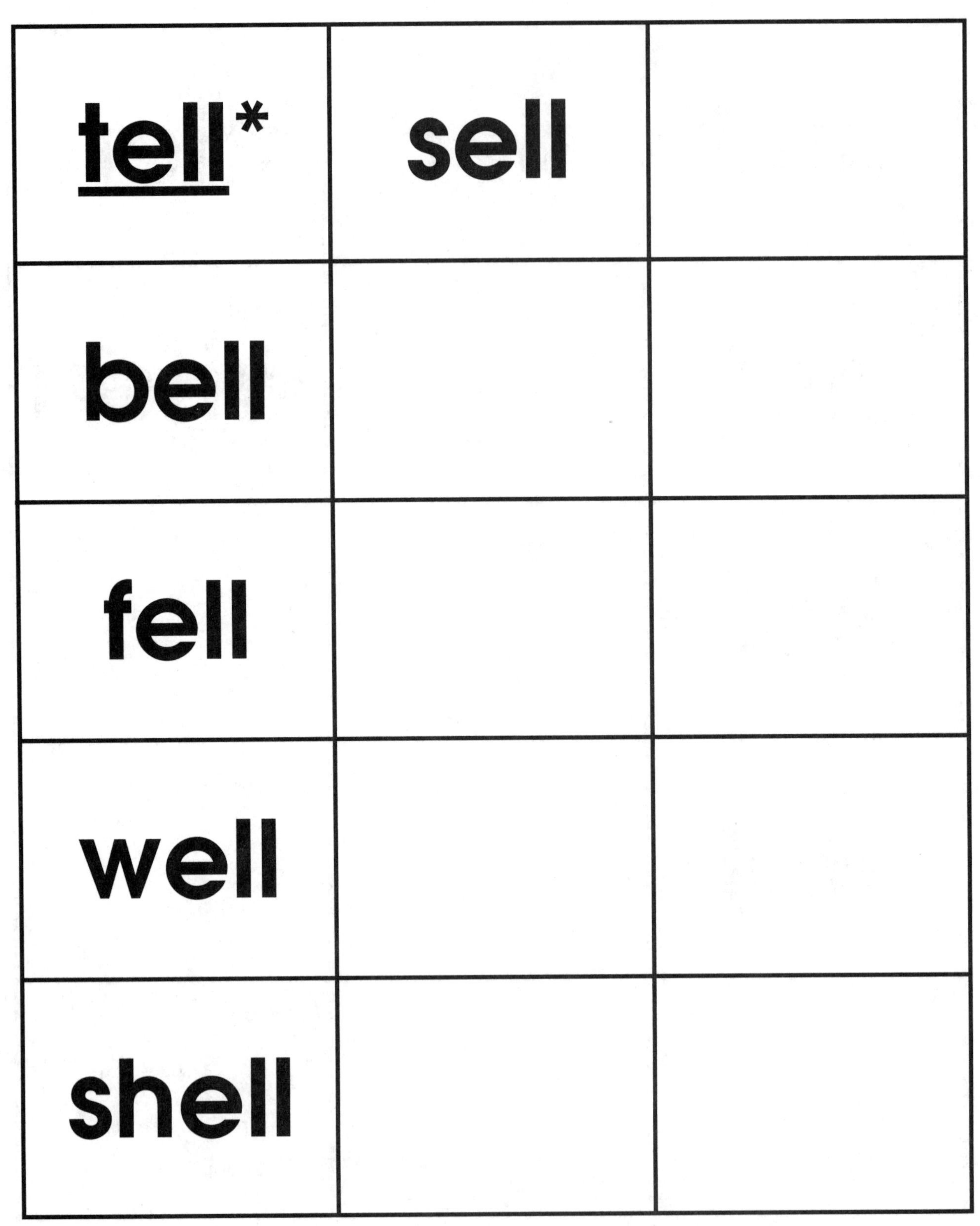

tell*	sell	
bell		
fell		
well		
shell		

SHORT-VOWEL CARDS

<u>bad</u>*	<u>pig</u>*	<u>mom</u>*
hat	win	hot
ran	hit	job
map	lip	top
mad	kid	hop

back	his	fox
had	sick	doll
has	pick	chop
that	ship	shop
glad	swim	drop

bus*	pet*	
cup	bed	
nut	let	
fun	red	
cut	web	

bug	tell	
but	less	
shut	then	
truck	bell	
must	shell	

VOWEL PATTERN CARDS—LEVELS 1 AND 2

A Patterns—Level 1

cat*	make*	car*
ran	lake	park
dad	race	hard
hat	tape	barn
cab	page	jar

A Patterns—Level 1

flat	same	card
clap	name	far
back	take	part
trap	gave	farm
that	shake	shark

A Patterns—Level 1

day*	clay	
say	stay	
may	play	
way	tray	
pay	stray	

A Patterns—Level 2

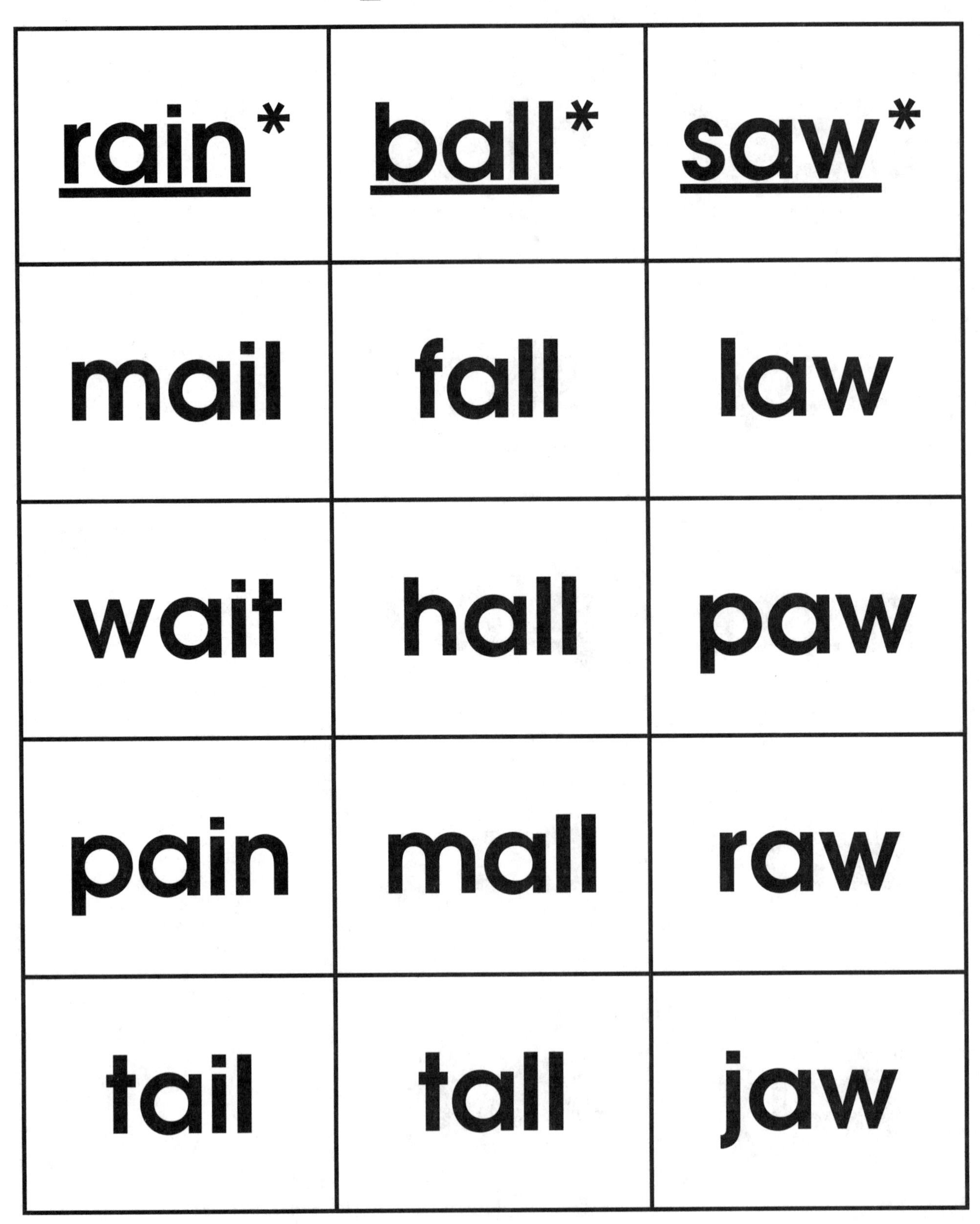

rain*	ball*	saw*
mail	fall	law
wait	hall	paw
pain	mall	raw
tail	tall	jaw

A Patterns—Level 2 (continued)

sail	wall	draw
paid	call	straw
gain	small	drawn
paint		
chain		

I Patterns—Level 1

hid*	ride*	girl*
lip	nice	dirt
win	bike	bird
big	five	sir
hit	mile	first

I Patterns—Level 1 (continued)

pin	side	shirt
fit	drive	third
kick	mine	thirst
swim	dime	firm
chin	wise	birth

I Patterns—Level 2

right*	by*	find*
night	my	mind
light	fly	kind
might	dry	blind
high	cry	mild

I Patterns—Level 2 (continued)

tight	sky	child
flight	shy	wild
bright	spy	grind
fight	try	climb

O Patterns—Level 1

mom*	rope*	go*
dot	note	no
job	hole	so
pot	nose	
top	coke	

O Patterns—Level 1(continued)

drop	hope	
lock	bone	
stop	code	
bomb	woke	
shock	spoke	

O Patterns—Level 1 (continued)

for*	boat*	look*
cord	coat	book
fork	moat	good
born	soap	foot
fort	load	stood

O Patterns—Level 1 (continued)

port	coal	hook
torn	soak	brook
sport	toast	wood
	float	
	coach	

O Patterns—Level 1 (continued)

cow*	crown	
how	tower	
town	owl	
plow		
brown		

O Vowel Patterns—Level 2

told*	**moon***	**boil***
cold	roof	coin
colt	pool	soil
gold	boot	point
fold	tool	noise

O Vowel Patterns—Level 2 (continued)

sold	shoot	spoil
hold	tooth	voice
mold	broom	

O Vowel Patterns—Level 2 (continued)

low*	loud*	boy*
row	south	toy
snow	sound	joy
grow	mouth	soy
show	shout	Roy

O Vowel Patterns—Level 2 (continued)

flow	count	
blow		

U Patterns Levels 1–2

mud*	cute*	hurt*
cup	use	curl
bus	tune	fur
fun	huge	burn
rug	June	turn

U Patterns Levels 1–2 (continued)

sun	fuse	nurse
bug	mule	curve
club	glue	purse

U Patterns Levels 1–2 (continued)

blue*		
true		
glue		
Sue		
clue		

E Patterns—Level 1

red*	feet*	her*
ten	deep	germ
beg	meet	herd
get	feel	clerk
bell	free	nerve

E Patterns—Level 1 (continued)

less	green	serve
next	seed	
left	need	
pet	queen	
step	jeep	

E Patterns—Level 2

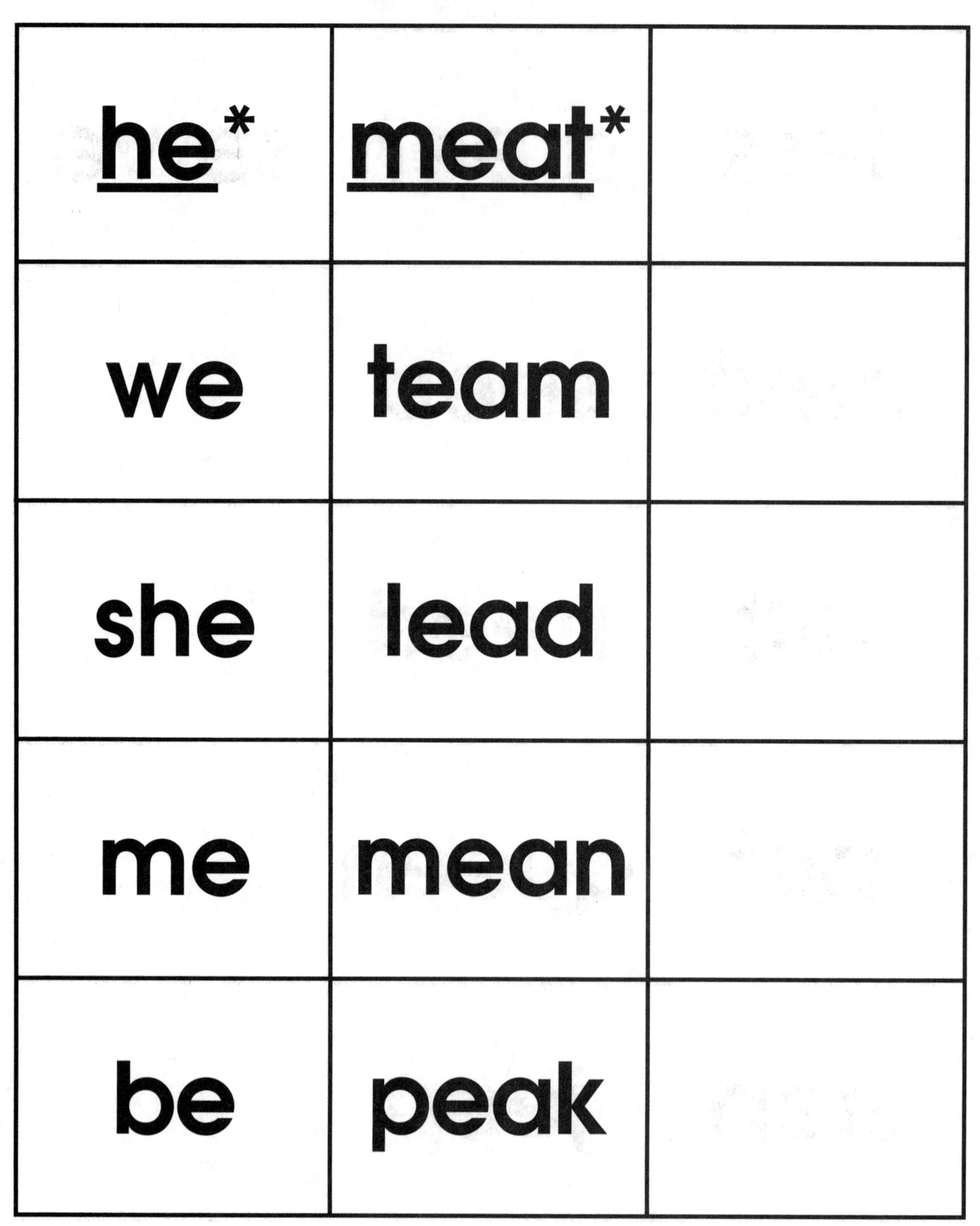

he*	meat*	
we	team	
she	lead	
me	mean	
be	peak	

<u>E</u> Patterns—Level 2 (continued)

clean	<u>head</u>*	<u>new</u>*
beat	lead	grew
dream	bread	few
beach	dead	chew
leaf	deaf	flew

E Patterns—Level 2 (continued)

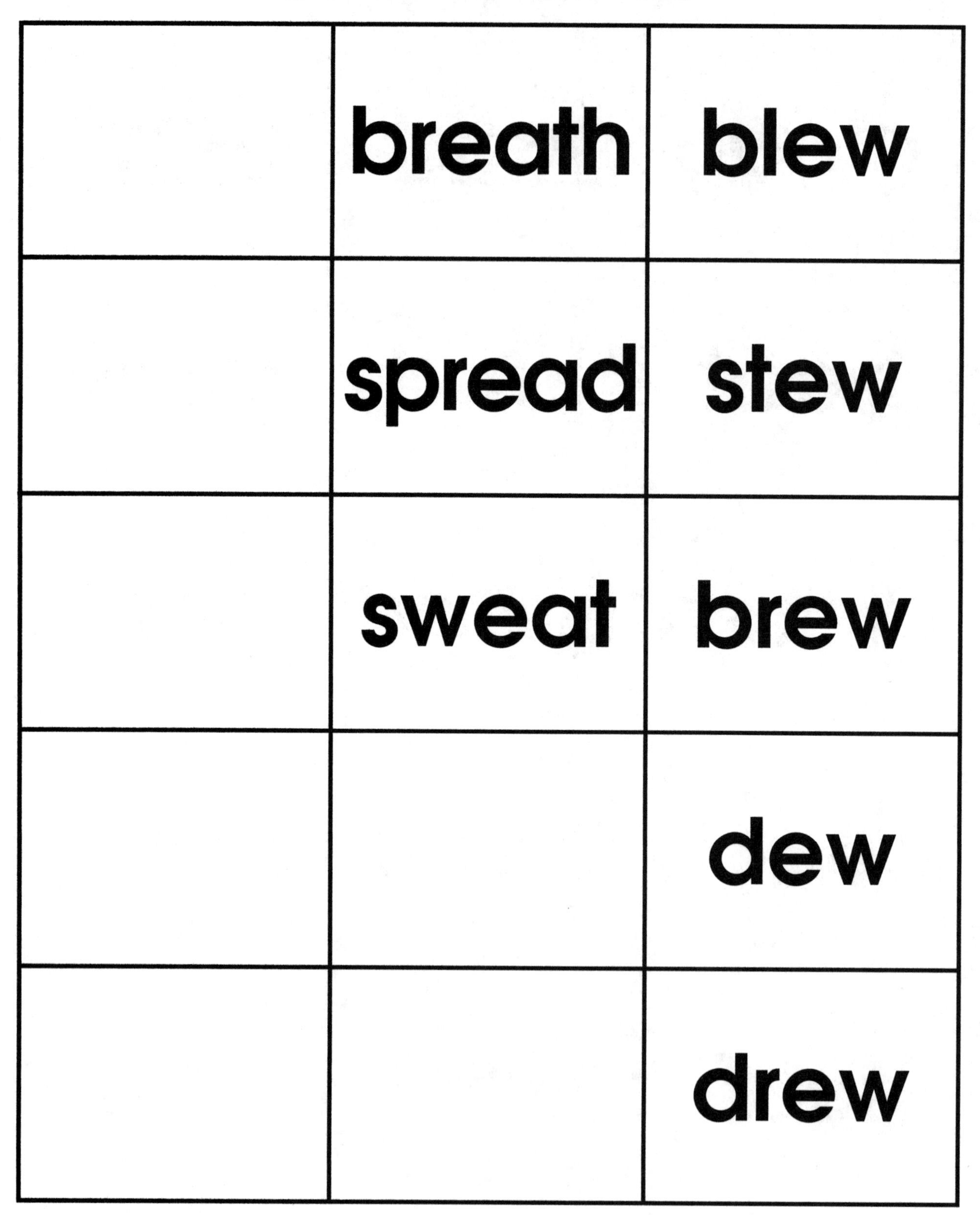

	breath	blew
	spread	stew
	sweat	brew
		dew
		drew

APPENDIX C

Word Scramble Activities, Cut-Up Sentences, and Dictation Sentences

WORD SCRAMBLE ACTIVITIES FOR STAGES 3, 4, AND 5

A Family

Letters: t, b, f, l, a, p, c, s

1. Make the word bat.
2. Change one letter to spell fat.
3. Change one letter to spell cat.
4. Change one letter to spell cap.
5. Change one letter to spell lap.
6. Add one letter to spell flap.
7. Change one letter to spell slap.
8. Change one letter to spell clap.

A Family

Letters: a, t, n, p, r, l, f, m

1. Make the word tap.
2. Change one letter to spell map.
3. Change one letter to spell mat.
4. Change one letter to spell fat.
5. Change one letter to spell fan.
6. Change one letter to spell ran.
7. Change one letter to spell pan.
8. Add one letter to spell plan.

I Family

Letters: i, s, t, g, p, f, w, n

1. Make the word sit.
2. Change one letter to spell fit.
3. Change one letter to spell fig.
4. Change one letter to spell pig.
5. Change one letter to spell wig.
6. Add one letter to spell twig.
7. Drop two letters, and add one letter to spell fig.
8. Change one letter to spell fin.

I Family

Letters: i, c, k, n, t, s, p, r, b

1. Make the word tick.
2. Add one letter to spell trick.
3. Change one letter to spell brick.
4. Drop two letters, and add one letter to spell pick.
5. Drop two letters, and add one letter to spell pin.
6. Change one letter to spell pit.
7. Change one letter to spell sit.
8. Change one letter to spell sip.

Combining A and I

Letters: a, i, f, g, b, w, t

1. Make the word fat.
2. Change one letter to spell fit.
3. Change one letter to spell fig.
4. Change one letter to spell big.
5. Drop one letter, and add two letters to spell twig.
6. Take one letter away to spell wig.
7. Change one letter to spell wag.
8. Change one letter to spell bag.

Combining A and I

Letters: a, i, c, k, t, r, b, p

1. Make the word pack.
2. Change one letter to spell pick.
3. Drop one letter, and add two letters to spell brick.
4. Drop two letters, and add one letter to spell tick.
5. Change one letter to spell tack.
6. Add one letter to spell track.
7. Drop one letter to spell rack.
8. Change one letter to spell back.

O Family

Letters: o, t, p, s, d, h, r, c

1. Make the word stop.
2. Drop one letter to spell top.
3. Change one letter to spell hop.
4. Change one letter to spell hot.
6. Add one letter to spell shot.
7. Drop two letters, and add a letter to spell dot.
8. Drop one letter, and add two letters to spell drop.
9. Drop two letters, and add one letter to spell cop.

O Family

Letters: o, c, k, l, r, s, b, n, k, c
(Note that you will need two k's and two c's for this activity.)

1. Make the word rob.
2. Drop one letter, and add two letters to spell rock.
3. Change one letter to spell lock.
4. Add one letter to spell block.
5. Drop two letters, and add one letter to spell sock.
6. Drop one letter, and add two letters to spell clock.
7. Drop two letters, and add two letters to spell knock.
8. Drop two letters, and add one letter to spell knob.

Combining A, I, and O

Letters: a, i, o, p, t, s

1. Make the word sit.
2. Change one letter to spell sat.
3. Change one letter to spell pat.
4. Change one letter to spell pot.
5. Add one letter to spell spot.
6. Change one letter to spell spit.
7. Drop one letter to spell sit.

Combining A, I, and O

Letters: a, o, i, c, k, r, s, t, l

1. Make the word sick.
2. Add one letter to spell stick.
3. Change one letter to spell stack.
4. Change one letter to spell stock.
5. Drop two letters, and add one letter to spell rock.
6. Change one letter to spell rack.
7. Change two letters to spell lick.
8. Change one letter to spell tick.

U Family

Letters: u, t, g, h, s, n, l, b

1. Make the word bug.
2. Change one letter to spell hug.
3. Change one letter to spell hut.
4. Add one letter to spell shut.
5. Change two letters to spell slug.
6. Drop two letters, and add one letter to spell gun.
7. Change one letter to spell sun.
8. Change one letter to spell bun.

U Family

Letters: u, c, k, s, t, r, n, g, d, f

1. Make the word fun.
2. Change one letter to spell sun.
3. Drop one letter, and add two letters to spell suck.
4. Add one letter to spell stuck.
5. Drop one letter, and spell tuck.
6. Add one letter to spell truck.
7. Drop two letters, and add one letter to spell duck.
8. Drop two letters, and add one letter to spell dug.

Combining A, I, O, and U

Letters: a, i, o, u, t, p, s, r, n

1. Make the word run.
2. Change one letter to spell ran.
3. Change one letter to spell rap.
4. Change one letter to spell rip.
5. Add two letters, and spell strip.
6. Drop one letter to spell trip.
7. Drop one letter to spell tip.
8. Change one letter to spell top.

Combining A, I, O, and U

Letters: i, o, u, s, p, g, t, b, a

1. Make the word but.
2. Change one letter to spell bit.
3. Change one letter to spell pit.
4. Add one letter to spell spit.
5. Change one letter to spell spot.
6. Drop one letter to spell pot.
7. Change one letter to spell pat.
8. Change one letter to spell bat.

E Family

Letters: e, d, h, p, r, s, t, l

1. Make the word pet.
2. Change one letter to spell let.
3. Change one letter to spell led.
4. Add one letter to spell sled.
5. Change one letter to spell shed.
6. Drop two letters, and add one letter to spell red.
7. Drop one letter, and add two letters to spell rest.
8. Change one letter to spell pest.

E Family

Letters: l, e, m, n, b, s, h, w, t, l
(Note that you will need two l's for this activity.)

1. Make the word sell.
2. Change one letter to spell bell.
3. Change one letter to spell tell.
4. Drop two letters, and add one letter to spell ten.
5. Add one letter to spell then.
6. Change one letter to spell when.
7. Drop one letter to spell hen.
8. Change one letter to spell men.

Combining A, I, O, U, and E

Letters: a, i, o, e, u, t, s, m, h

1. Make the word mat.
2. Change one letter to spell met.
3. Change one letter to spell mit.
4. Change one letter to spell hit.
5. Change one letter to spell hot.
6. Add one letter to spell shot.
7. Change one letter to spell shut.
8. Drop one letter to spell hut.

Combining A, I, O, U, and E

Letters: a, i, o, u, c, k, t, r, b, l

1. Make the word back.
2. Add one letter to spell black.
3. Change one letter to spell block.
4. Drop one letter, and change one letter to spell lick.
5. Change one letter to spell luck.
6. Change one letter to spell tuck.
7. Add one letter to spell truck.
8. Drop two letters, and add one letter to spell buck.

Short Vowels (mixed)

Letters: a, e, i, s, p, l, d, c

1. Make the word led.
2. Add one letter to spell sled.
3. Change one letter to spell slid.
4. Change one letter to spell slip.
5. Change one letter to spell slap.
6. Change one letter to spell clap.
7. Change one letter to spell clip.
8. Drop one letter to spell lip.

Short Vowels (mixed)

Letters: o, u, c, k, h, i, t, s, g

1. Make the word kit.
2. Change one letter to spell hit.
3. Change one letter to spell hot.
4. Add one letter to spell shot.
5. Change one letter to spell shut.
6. Change two letters to spell chug.
7. Drop one letter to spell hug.
8. Change one letter to spell tug.

A Patterns—Level 1

Letters: a, e, r, t, d, p, g, y

1. Make the word drag.
2. Drop one letter to spell rag.
3. Add one letter to spell rage.
4. Change one letter to spell page.
5. Drop two letters, and add one letter to spell pay.
6. Change one letter to spell ray.
7. Add one letter to spell tray.

A Patterns—Level 1

Letters: a, e, r, t, m, k, c, g

1. Make the word make.
2. Drop one letter, and add one letter to spell mark.
3. Drop two letters, and add two letters to spell cart.
4. Drop one letter to spell car.
5. Drop one letter, and add two letters to spell cake.
6. Change one letter to spell cage.
7. Change one letter to spell rage.
8. Drop one letter to spell rag.

A Vowel Patterns—Level 2

Letters: a, i, l, t, n, s, m, c, h, l
(Note that you will need two l's for this activity.)

1. Make the word tall.
2. Change one letter to spell mall.
3. Add one letter to spell small.
4. Drop two letters, and add one letter to spell mail.
5. Change one letter to spell main.
6. Drop one letter, and add two letters to spell chain.
7. Change two letters to spell stain.

A Vowel Patterns—Level 2

Letters: a, w, i, r, s, t, d, n, p

1. Make the word raw.
2. Add one letter to spell draw.
3. Add one letter to spell drawn.
4. Change one letter to spell drain.
5. Drop one letter, and add two letters to spell sprain.
6. Drop two letters to spell rain.
7. Add two letters to spell strain.

I Patterns—Level 1

Letters: i, d, r, t, h, s, e, p, n, b

1. Make the word tin.
2. Change one letter to spell pin.
3. Add one letter to spell pine.
4. Drop one letter, and add two letters to spell shine.
5. Drop two letters, and add one letter to spell dine.
6. Drop two letters, and add two letters to spell dirt.
7. Change one letter, and add one letter to spell birth.

I Patterns—Level 1

Letters: i, r, t, d, n, f, s, m, v, e, h

1. Make the word first.
2. Drop two letters, and add one letter to spell firm.
3. Drop two letters, and add two letters to spell five.
4. Change one letter to spell dive.
5. Add one letter to spell drive.
6. Drop two letters, and add one letter to spell dime.
7. Drop two letters, and add three letters to spell shine.
8. Drop two letters, and add one letter to spell mine.

I Patterns—Level 2

Letters: m, y, b, i, n, d, g, h, t, r

1. Make the word my.
2. Change one letter to spell by.
3. Drop one letter, and add three letters to spell bind.
4. Change one letter to spell mind.
5. Drop two letters, and add three letters to spell might.
6. Change one letter to spell night.
7. Drop one letter, and add two letters to spell bright.

I Patterns—Level 2

Letters: c, r, y, d, f, l, i, g, h, t

1. Make the word cry.
2. Change one letter to spell dry.
3. Change two letters to spell fly.
4. Drop two letters, and add three letters to spell fight.
5. Add one letter to spell flight.
6. Drop one letter to spell light.
7. Drop two letters, and add one letter to spell right.

<u>O</u> Patterns—Level 1

Letters: o, p, d, s, a, t, g, w, o
(Note that you will need two o's for this activity.)

1. Make the word <u>stop</u>.
2. Drop on letter, and add one letter to spell <u>soap</u>.
3. Change two letters to spell <u>toad</u>.
4. Change one letter, and add one letter to spell <u>stood</u>.
5. Drop two letters, and add one letter to spell <u>good</u>.
6. Change one letter to spell <u>wood</u>.

<u>O</u> Patterns—Level 1

Letters: o, p, s, t, d, a, c, k, e, w, h, c
(Note that you will need two c's for this activity.)

1. Make the word <u>so</u>.
2. Add two letters to spell <u>soak</u>.
3. Change two letters to spell <u>coat</u>.
4. Drop one letter, and add two letters to spell <u>coach</u>.
5. Drop three letters, and add two letters to spell <u>code</u>.
6. Change one letter to spell <u>coke</u>.
7. Drop one letter, and add two letters to spell <u>spoke</u>.
8. Drop two letters, and add one letter to spell <u>woke</u>.

O Patterns—Level 2

Letters: c, o, l, d, h, w, r, g, n

1. Make the word cold.
2. Change one letter to spell hold.
3. Drop two letters, and add one letter to spell how.
4. Change one letter to spell cow.
5. Add two letters to spell crown.
6. Drop two letters to spell row.
7. Add one letter to spell grow.

O Patterns—Level 2

Letters: b, o, y, j, i, h, l, t, n, s, o
(Note that you will need two o's for this activity.)

1. Make the word boy.
2. Change one letter to spell joy.
3. Drop one letter, and add two letters to spell join.
4. Change two letters to spell boil.
5. Change two letters to spell boot.
6. Drop one letter, and add two letters to spell shoot.
7. Drop one letter to spell hoot.

U Patterns—Levels 1–2

Letters: u, n, e, l, r, t, g, h

1. Make the word rug.
2. Change one letter to spell hug.
3. Add one letter to spell huge.
4. Change two letters to spell tune.
5. Drop one letter, and add one letter to spell true.
6. Change two letters to spell glue.
7. Drop two letters, and add one letter to spell gun.
8. Change one letter to spell run.

U Patterns—Levels 1–2

Letters: e, u, t, r, n, l, f, b, s

1. Make the word fur.
2. Change one letter, and add one letter to spell burn.
3. Change one letter to spell turn.
4. Change two letters, and add one letter to spell nurse.
5. Drop two letters to spell use.
6. Add one letter to spell fuse.
7. Drop one letter, and add two letters to spell flute.
8. Drop three letters, and add one letter to spell fun.

E Patterns—Level 1

Letters: m, e, r, h, d, t, s, v, e
(Note that you will need two e's for this activity.)

1. Make the word me.
2. Add two letters to spell meet.
3. Change two letters to spell seed.
4. Drop one letter, and add two letters to spell serve.
5. Drop three letters, and add two letters to spell herd.
6. Drop one letter to spell her.

E Patterns—Level 1

Letters: e, s, l, b, d, g, r, h, n, e
(Note that you will need two e's for this activity.)

1. Make the word sled.
2. Drop one letter, and add two letters to spell bleed.
3. Change three letters to spell green.
4. Drop one letter, and change two letters to spell seed.
5. Drop two letters, and add one letter to spell she.
6. Drop one letter to spell he.

E Patterns—Level 2

Letters: s, h, e, a, d, b, r, t, w

1. Make the word she.
2. Drop one letter to spell he.
3. Add two letters to spell head.
4. Drop one letter, and add two letters to spell bread.
5. Drop one letter, and add two letters to spell breath.
6. Drop three letters, and add two letters to spell sweat.

E Patterns—Level 2

Letters: n, e, w, c, h, b, r, a, t, d

1. Make the word new.
2. Drop one letter, and add two letters to spell chew.
3. Change two letters to spell brew.
4. Drop one letter, and add two letters to spell bread.
5. Drop one letter, and add two letters to spell thread.
6. Drop two letters to spell read.

E Patterns—Level 2

Letters: e, t, a, b, g, w, h, s, c, d

1. Make the word be.
2. Add one letter to spell beg.
3. Drop one letter, and add two letters to spell beat.
4. Drop one letter, and add two letters to spell beach.
5. Drop two letters, and add one letter to spell bead.
6. Drop two letters, and add three letters to spell wheat.
7. Drop one letter to spell heat.
8. Drop one letter, and add one letter to spell seat.

E Patterns—Level 2

Letters: e, r, a, p, s, l, d, t, f, e
(Note that you will need two e's for this activity.)

1. Make the word seed.
2. Change two letters to spell seat.
3. Change two letters to spell deaf.
4. Change one letter to spell leaf.
5. Change one letter to spell lead.
6. Drop one letter, and add three letters to spell spread.
7. Drop two letters to spell read.
8. Drop one letter to spell red.

CUT-UP SENTENCES FOR STAGE 2

BSM Word Study Cut-Up Sentences

A	bunny	is	soft	.
A	bear	is	mean	.
A	monkey	is	brown	.
A	boy	is	small	.
A	snake	is	black	.
The	match	can	burn	.
The	man	can	swim	.
The	boy	can	swing	.
The	bird	can	sing	.
The	ball	can	bounce	.

CFD Word Study Cut-Up Sentences

I	can	draw	a	fat	cat	.
The	cat	and	dog	are	friends	.
A	duck	can	swim	fast	.	
Do	you	like	to	catch	fish	?
A	frog	can	eat	flies	.	
I	can	dance	with	my	friend	.
I	can	play	the	big	drum	.
Fred	went	fishing	in	the	creek	.
Can	you	find	my	dog	?	
We	had	cake	for	my	birthday	.

TRL Word Study Cut-Up Sentences

Tommy	ran	to	the	lake	.	
He	finished	the	race	last	.	
Let	me	rake	the	leaves	.	
We	looked	for	the	tractor	.	
The	little	rabbit	was	lazy	.	
I	am	learning	to	read	.	
The	lion	roared	at	the	tiger	.
Please	turn	on	the	light	.	
My	teacher	likes	to	read	.	
He	rode	on	a	train	.	

NPW Word Study Cut-Up Sentences

I	have	a	new	puppy	.	
We	like	to	play	tag	.	
She	has	a	new	watch	.	
Will	you	play	with	me	?	
William	is	a	nice	pony	.	
They	want	to	make	popcorn	.	
Never	play	with	fire	!		
Please	water	the	new	plant	.	
She	has	nine	new	pennies	.	
I	have	a	new	purple	watch	.

GHJ Word Study Cut-Up Sentences

Henry	had	grapes	for	lunch	.		
We	had	a	jack-	o'-	lantern	.	
Gorillas	like	to	eat	bananas	.		
Grasshoppers	have	long	legs	.			
The	glass	was	full	of	juice	.	
Helicopters	fly	high	in	the	sky	.	
The	horse	got	out	of	the	gate	.
The	girl	had	a	heavy	jacket	.	
I	jumped	in	the	grass	.		
Have	you	got	a	jump- rope	?		

ZKV Word Study Cut-Up Sentences

Kangaroos	live	at	the	zoo	•		
I	have	a	zipper	in	my	vest	•
Kites	fly	very	high	•			
The	zebra	kicked	his	hoof	•		
I	will	keep	my	valentines	•		
The	vacuum	is	in	the	kitchen	•	
My	kitten	broke	the	vase	•		
We	saw	a	video	on	zebras	•	
The	king	played	the	violin	•		
The	zoo-keeper	has	a	key	•		

DICTATION SENTENCES

A Word Family

1. The man has a black hat.
2. He took a nap on a mat.
3. She put her hat on the rack.
4. I will step on a tack.
5. I can clap my hands.
6. We have a snack in a sack.
7. I ran on the track.
8. We cook fish in a pan.
9. The map led us back.
10. We got a new black van.

I Word Family

1. Sit on the big brick.
2. There was a tick on my dog.
3. She has a wig on her head.
4. I like to dig a pit.
5. The house is made of brick.
6. We can pick up a big stick.
7. He will play a trick on me.
8. He got hit with a stick.
9. His skin got hot in the sun.
10. The rat bit my chin.

O Family

1. The pot was very hot.
2. We did not see a fox.
3. Bob ran to his job.
4. She does not like corn on the cob.
5. I saw a man rob a bank.
6. Please stop, and lock the van.
7. There was a spot on his chin.
8. She likes to shop at the mall.
9. My mom will mop the floor.
10. The clock will not stop.

U Family

1. The black bug fell on my foot.
2. The yellow duck has two feet.
3. We have fun when we play tag.
4. The sun was hot today.
5. A truck was in the mud.
6. The yellow duck likes to cluck.
7. I put my hot dog on a bun.
8. He ran fast but lost the race.
9. The truck got stuck in the mud.
10. The gun made a loud pop.

E Family

1. I got a new pet cat.
2. I fed the rat in the shed.
3. We led the pig to the shed.
4. The men sell wet shells.
5. We had 10 men in the well.
6. She fell into a dark well.
7. The school bell will ring soon.
8. Mom let us sled in the snow.
9. Please let me ride on the jet.
10. My teacher likes to tell stories.

A Patterns—Level 1

1. Dad made a trap for the shark.
2. We will play a card game.
3. It is hard to chase a snake.
4. I had the same hat as my mom.
5. Turn the page in the big book.
6. Park your car beside the barn.
7. The police will chase the robbers.
8. We play at the park near the lake.
9. We put the jam in a jar.
10. We will name our new cat Max.

A Patterns—Level 2

1. May we go to the mall and shop?
2. We had to wait for the train.
3. I saw a man paint the wall.
4. I like to draw on the wall.
5. I sail on a small boat.
6. The boy drank his milk with a straw.
7. Please stay out of the rain.
8. The boy got a small train.
9. The paint made a stain on the wall.
10. We walked down the long hall.

I Patterns—Level 1

1. He hit a ball to the girl.
2. Do not ride your bike in the dirt.
3. The bird cannot swim.
4. I wore my shirt on the trip.
5. This side of my chin is red.
6. I can kick when I swim.
7. Write your name with this pen.
8. He hit the side of the bird.
9. Please shine your shoes before the trip.
10. I found a dime in the dirt.

I Patterns—Level 2

1. I will help the girl find her mom.
2. The wild monkey likes to climb trees.
3. The light will blind the man.
4. What kind of bird is in the cage?
5. He rode a bike on his first try.
6. The little child will try her best.
7. She might fly her kite first.
8. I had to buy my first bike.
9. My shirt is too tight.
10. I told the child not to cry.

O Patterns—Level 1

1. She wrote a note to the coach.
2. I like to read a good book.
3. He likes to float in the brook.
4. We will chop wood for the fire.
5. The shock of the bomb woke us up.
6. I will eat my toast with a fork.
7. He put the coke on top of the desk.
8. I broke a bone in my nose.
9. She will soak her foot in the brook.
10. Drop the note in my box.

O Patterns—Level 2

1. I wore my boots to town.
2. The boy can shoot an owl.
3. I will shout for joy!
4. Show me the way to town.
5. The king's crown is in the tower.
6. We have a new brown colt.
7. Count the brown cows in the barn.
8. Count the coins in this box.
9. I live south of town.
10. We found a pot of gold on the roof.

U Patterns—Levels 1–2

1. Sue is a good nurse.
2. June bugs are fun to find.
3. The bus went around a curve.
4. I dropped glue on the rug.
5. The mule has soft fur.
6. The club took a trip on the bus.
7. She had a huge purse.
8. We have fun in our club.
9. Mom hung the rug out to dry.
10. He will glue the rug to the floor.

E Patterns—Level 1

1. She rode in a red jeep.
2. She will help me serve the food.
3. I left my pet at home.
4. The mother bird left her nest.
5. The queen will free her slaves.
6. The clerk left the store.
7. We will sled in the snow.
8. We rode the jeep in the deep snow.
9. He helped me plant the seeds.
10. The herd of deer ran free.

E Patterns—Level 2

1. I dream about going to the beach.
2. I grew wheat in the field.
3. We ate bread with the stew.
4. Please clean your room.
5. The wind blew in the trees.
6. My ball team won the game.
7. The leaf blew down the street.
8. I beat my brother in the race.
9. I spread butter on my bread.
10. The bird flew to the beach.

APPENDIX D

Auxiliary Instructional Materials

WATCH OUR SIGHT WORDS GROW

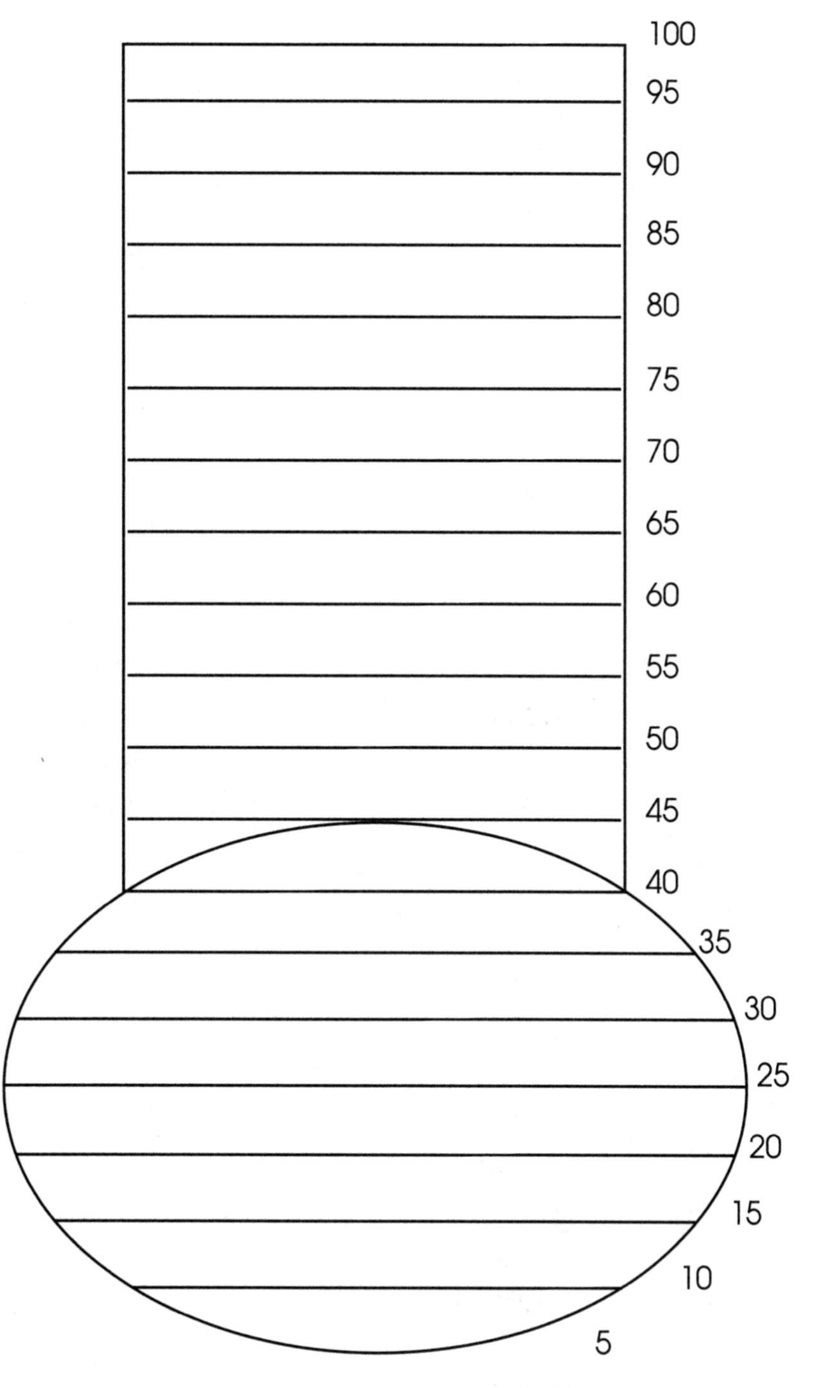

100 MOST FREQUENT WORDS IN BOOKS FOR BEGINNING READERS

the
a
and
to
I
in
is
on
you
it
of
said
can
for
my
but
all
we
are
up
at
with
me
they
have
he
out
that
one
big
go
was
like

what
not
do
then
this
no
too
she
went
see
will
so
some
down
little
come
get
be
now
when
there
into
day
look
eat
make
his
here
your
an
back
mom
dog

very
did
her
from
had
got
put
came
just
cat
them
tree
where
away
time
as
water
home
made
long
has
help
good
going
by
how
house
dad
or
two
red
am
over
saw

Bodrova, E., Leong, D.J., & Semenov, D. (1998). *100 most frequent words in books for beginning readers.* Aurora, CO: McREL.

READING LOG

Title: ____

Author: ______________________ Illustrator: ______________________

Draw a picture of your favorite part of the story.

Write a sentence about your favorite part of the story.

____

....

____

____

....

____

LISTENING CENTER LOG

Name ______________________________________

Date ______________________________________

I listened to ______________________________________

This is a picture of my favorite part.

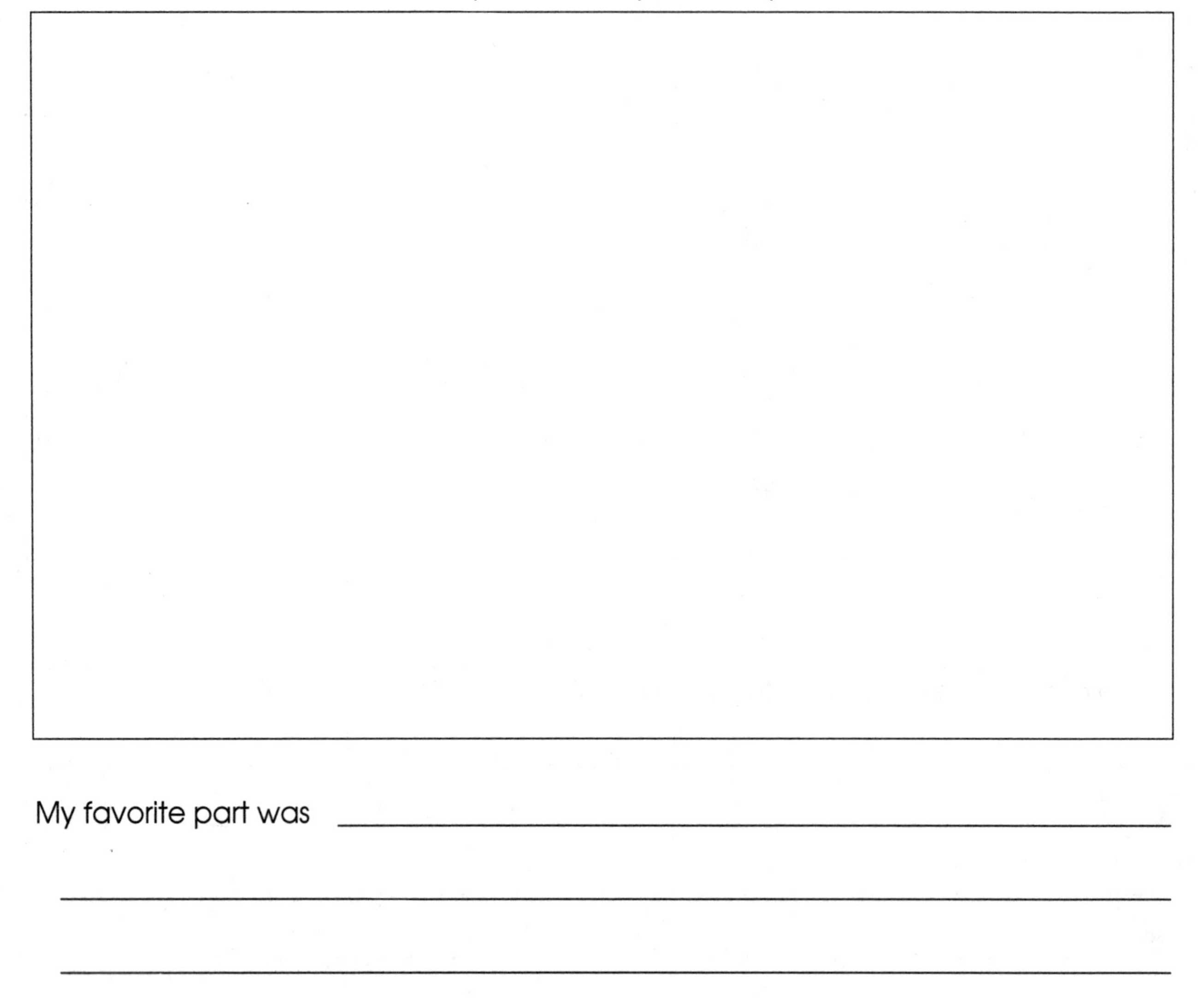

My favorite part was ______________________________________

____

____

____

WORD STUDY LOG

Name ________________________________

1. ALPHABET	DATE	2. BEGINNING CONSONANTS	DATE

3. WORD FAMILIES	DATE	4. VOWEL PATTERNS	DATE

WORD BANK (optional)

WORD STUDY CARD SORTING

WORD SORT INSTRUCTIONS AND SEQUENCE

Instruction Summary

1. Header cards must be known words or pictures.
2. No more than three columns.
3. No more than four words in column.
4. Place word first, then read the column so that word pattern assists the student.
5. When student can sort on own with little assistance, reinforce with spelling and by playing Concentration and Word Scramble.
6. When group can recognize most words randomly presented, group is ready to move on.

Instructional Sequence

Stage 1: Letter and Picture Sorts

1. Letter recognition
2. Picture sorting
3. Picture and letter sorting

Stage 2: Word Families

1. Short *a* families: *cat man cap*—drop one, and add *back* family
2. Short *i* families: *hit big win*—drop one, and add *sick* family
3. Review *a* and *i* families together
4. Short *o* families: *hot top job*—drop one, and add *sock* family

   Review a's, i's, o's. If student is quite adept, skip the short *e* and *u* word families and go straight to the short-vowel groups. If word families have been a struggle, complete the short *e* and *u* families. These will probably go quickly.
5. Short *u* families: *cut bug run*—drop one, and add *duck* family
6. Short *e* families: *pet red hen*—drop one, and add *tell* family

Stage 3: Short Vowels

1. Short *a*, *o*, and *i* vowels; no longer in families: *bad pig mom*
2. Drop one short vowel pattern, and add the u's: *bad mom bus*
3. Drop one short vowel pattern, and add the e's: *bad bus pet*

Stage 4: Vowel Patterns—Level I

1. *cat make car*—drop one, and add *day* pattern
2. *hid ride girl*
3. *mom rope go*
4. *for boat look cow*
5. *red feet her*—drop one and add h

Stage 5: Vowel Patterns—Level 2

1. *rain ball saw*
2. *right by find*
3. *told moon boil*
4. *low loud boy*
5. *meat head new*

REFERENCES

Adams, M.J. (1990). *Beginning to read: Thinking and learning about print*. Cambridge, MA: MIT Press.

Allington, R.L. (1977). If they don't read much, how they ever gonna get good? *Journal of Reading, 21*, 57–61.

Anderson, R.C., Mason, J., & Shirey, L. (1984). The reading group: An experimental investigation of a labyrinth. *Reading Research Quarterly, 20*, 6–38.

Bean, W., & Bouffler, C. (1997). *Read, write, spell*. York, ME: Stenhouse.

Betts, E.A. (1946). *Foundations of reading instruction*. New York: American Book.

Bodrova, E., Leong, D.J., & Semenov, D. (1998). *100 most frequent words in books for beginning readers*. Aurora, CO: McREL.

Butler, D., & Clay, M.M. (1982). *Reading begins at home: Preparing children before they go to school*. Exeter, NH: Heinemann.

Chall, J.S. (1967). *Learning to read: The great debate; an inquiry into the science, art, and ideology of old and new methods of teaching children to read 1910–1965*. New York: McGraw-Hill.

Chall, J.S. (1987). The importance of instruction in reading methods for all teachers. In R.F. Bowler (Ed.), *Intimacy with language: A forgotten basic in teacher education* (pp. 15–23). Baltimore: Orton Dyslexic Society.

Chomsky, C. (1978). When you still can't read in third grade: After decoding what? In S.J. Samuels (Ed.), *What research has to say about reading instruction* (pp. 13–30). Newark, DE: International Reading Association.

Clay, M.M. (1979). *Reading: The patterning of complex behaviour*. Auckland, New Zealand: Heinemann.

Clay, M.M. (1985). *The early detection of reading difficulties* (3rd ed.). Portsmouth, NH: Heinemann.

Clay, M.M. (1993). *Reading recovery: A guidebook for teachers in training*. Portsmouth, NH: Heinemann.

Darling-Hammond, L., & Goodwin, L.A. (1993). A progress towards professionalism in teaching. In G. Cawelti (Ed.), *Challenges and achievements of American education* (pp. 19–52). Alexandria, VA: Association for Supervision and Curriculum Development.

Dowhower, S.L. (1987). Effects of repeated reading on second grade transitional readers' fluency and comprehension. *Reading Research Quarterly, 22*, 289–406.

Flesch, R. (1955). *Why Johnny can't read—And what you can do about it*. New York: Harper & Row.

Fountas, I.C., & Pinnell, G.S. (1996). *Guided reading: Good first teaching for all children*. Portsmouth, NH: Heinemann.

Gill, J.T. (1992). The relationship between word recognition and spelling. In S. Templeton & D. Bear (Eds.), *Development of orthographic knowledge and the foundations of literacy* (pp. 79–104). Hillsdale, NJ: Erlbaum.

Henderson, E. (1990). *Teaching spelling* (2nd ed.). Boston: Houghton Mifflin.

Herman, P.A. (1985). The effects of repeated readings on reading rate, speech pauses, and word recognition accuracy. *Reading Research Quarterly, 20*, 553–565.

Juel, C. (1988). Learning to read and write: A longitudinal study of fifty-four children from first through fourth grade. *Journal of Educational Psychology, 80*, 437–447.

Keene, E.O., & Zimmermann, S. (1997). *Mosaic of thought: Teaching comprehension in a reader's workshop*. Portsmouth, NH: Heinemann.
LaBerge, D., & Samuels, S.J. (1974). Toward a theory of automatic information processing in reading. *Cognitive Psychology, 6*, 293–323.
Learning First Alliance. (1998). *Every child reading: An action plan*. Washington, DC: Author.
Lombardino, L., Defillipo, F., Sarisky, C., & Montgomery, A. (1992, June). *Kindergarten children's performance on the Early Reading Screening Instrument*. Paper presented at the annual convention of the American Speech-Language-Hearing Association, San Antonio, TX.
Morris, D. (1993). *A selective history of the Howard Street Tutoring Program (1979–1989)* (Report No. SC011220). Chicago: Chicago Public Schools. (ERIC Document Reproduction Service No. ED355473)
Morris, D. (1998). Assessing printed word knowledge in beginning readers: The Early Reading Screening Instrument (ERSI). *Illinois Reading Council Journal, 26*(2), 30–39.
Morris, D. (1999). *The Howard Street tutoring manual: Teaching at-risk readers in the primary grades*. New York: Guilford.
Morris, D., & Perney, J. (1984). Developmental spelling as a predictor of first-grade reading achievement. *The Elementary School Journal, 84*(4), 441–457.
Morris, D., Tyner, B., & Perney, J. (2000). Early Steps: Replicating the effects of a first-grade reading intervention program. *Journal of Educational Psychology, 92*(4), 681–693.
National Institute of Child Health and Human Development. (2000). *Report of the National Reading Panel. Teaching children to read: An evidence-based assessment of the scientific research literature on reading and its implications for reading instruction* (NIH Publication No. 00-4769). Washington, DC: U.S. Government Printing Office.
Oxford Illustrated American Dictionary. (1998). New York: Oxford University Press.
Perfetti, C.A., & Lesgold, A.M. (1979). Coding and comprehension in skilled reading and implications for reading instruction. In L.B. Resnick & P.A. Weaver (Eds.), *Theory and practice of early reading* (pp. 57–84). Hillsdale, NJ: Erlbaum.
Perney, J., Morris, D., & Carter, S. (1997). Factorial and predictive validity of first graders' scores on the Early Reading Screening Instrument. *Psychological Reports, 81*, 207–210.
Rasinski, T., & Reinking, D. (1988). Redefining the role of reading fluency. *Georgia Journal of Reading, 13*(1), 21–27.
Reitsma, P. (1988). Reading practice for beginners: Effects of guided reading, reading-while-listening, and independent reading with computer-based reading feedback. *Reading Research Quarterly, 23*, 219–235.
Rosenshine, B. (1978). Academic engaged time, content covered, and direct instruction. *Journal of Education, 160*, 38–66.
Samuels, S.J. (1979). The method of repeated readings. *The Reading Teacher, 32*, 403–408.
Samuels, S.J., & Kamil, M.L. (1984). Models of the reading process. In P.D. Pearson (Ed.), *Handbook of reading research* (pp. 185–224). White Plains, NY: Longman.
Samuels, S.J., & LaBerge, D. (1983). A critique of a theory of automaticity in reading. Looking back: A retrospective analysis of the LaBerge-Samuels reading model. In L.M. Gentile, M.L. Kamil, & J. Blanchard (Eds.), *Reading research revisited* (pp. 39–55). Westerville, OH: Merrill.
Santa, C.M. (1999). *Early Steps: Learning from a reader*. Kalispell, MT: Scott.
Santa, C.M., & Hoien, T. (1999). An assessment of Early Steps: A program for early intervention of reading problems. *Reading Research Quarterly, 34*, 54–79.
Stanovich, K.E. (1986). Matthew Effects in reading: Some consequences of individual differences in the acquisition of literacy. *Reading Research Quarterly, 21*, 360–407.

Texas Reading Initiative: Differentiated Instruction. (n.d.) Retrieved October 27, 2002, from http://www.tea.state.tx.us/reading/model/diffinst.html
Vygotsky, L.S. (1978). *Mind in society: The development of higher psychological processes* (M. Cole, V. John-Steiner, S. Scribner, & E. Souberman, Eds. and Trans.). Cambridge, MA: Harvard University Press. (Original work published 1934)
Webster's Ninth New Collegiate Dictionary. (1984). Springfield, MA: Merriam-Webster.

Children's Literature References

Clough, M. (2000). *Monkey on the roof*. Ill. N.C. Lewis. Barrington, IL: Rigby.
Eggleton, J. (1999). *Cat's diary*. Ill. K. Hawley. Barrington, IL: Rigby.
Giles, J. (2001). *Brown Mouse plays a trick*. Ill. P. DeWitt-Grush. Barrington, IL: Rigby.
Melser, J. (1998). *My home*. Ill. I. Lowe. Bothell, WA: Wright Group.
Randell, B. (1994a). *A friend for Little White Rabbit*. Ill. D. Aitken. Barrington, IL: Rigby.
Randell, B. (1994b). *Honey for Baby Bear*. Ill. I. Lowe. Barrington, IL: Rigby.
Randell, B. (1997a). *The busy beavers*. Ill. M. Gardiner. Barrington, IL: Rigby.
Randell, B. (1997b). *Jessica in the dark*. Ill. L. McClelland. Barrington, IL: Rigby.
Randell, B. (2000). *Baby Panda*. Ill. M. Power. Barrington, IL: Rigby.
Russell-Arnot, E. (1999). *Bats*. Barrington, IL: Rigby.
Smith, A., Giles, J., & Randell, B. (2000a). *Big sea animals*. Barrington, IL: Rigby.
Smith, A., Giles, J., & Randell, B. (2000b). *Playing outside*. Photo. J. Pettitt. Barrington, IL: Rigby.

INDEX

A

B

C

D

E

F

G

H

I–J

K–L

M

N

O

P–Q

R

S

T–U

V

W–Z